T0153933

Birds *of* Ohio

Field Guide

Stan Tekiela

Adventure Publications
Cambridge, Minnesota

Dedication

To my wife, Katherine, and daughter, Abigail, with all my love

Acknowledgments

Many thanks to the National Wildlife Refuge System along with state and local agencies, both public and private, for stewarding the lands that are critical to the many bird species we so love.

Edited by Sandy Livoti, Brett Ortler and Kate Johnson

Cover, book design and illustrations by Jonathan Norberg

Range maps produced by Anthony Hertzel

Cover photo: Blue Jay by Stan Tekiela
All photos by Stan Tekiela except p. 282 (juvenile) by **Rick and Nora Bowers**; pp. 38 (soaring), 204 (female), 198 (female) by **Kevin T. Karlson**; pp. 44 (female) and 304 by **Maslowski Wildlife Productions**; p. 232 (displaying) by **Hartmut Walter**; pp. 38 (juvenile), 40 (juvenile), 144 (both juveniles), 148 (both juveniles), 240 (juvenile) and 242 (in-flight juvenile) by **Brian K. Wheeler**; and pp. 148 (male), 182 (female), 234 (main) and 294 (female) by **Jim Zipp**

To the best of the publisher's knowledge, all photos were of live birds. Some were photographed in a controlled condition.

15 14 13 12 11 10 9

Birds of Ohio Field Guide
First Edition 1999
Second Edition 2004
Third Edition 2020
Copyright © 1999, 2004 and 2020 by Stan Tekiela
Published by Adventure Publications
An imprint of AdventureKEEN
310 Garfield Street South
Cambridge, Minnesota 55008
(800) 678-7006
www.adventurepublications.net
All rights reserved
Printed in China
ISBN 978-1-59193-961-0 (pbk.); ISBN 978-1-59193-962-7 (ebook)

TABLE OF CONTENTS

WHAT'S NEW?

It is hard to believe that it's been more than 20 years since the debut of *Birds of Ohio Field Guide*. This critically acclaimed field guide has helped countless people identify and enjoy the birds that we love. Now, in this expanded third edition, *Birds of Ohio Field Guide* has many new and exciting changes and a fresh look, while retaining the same familiar, easy-to-use format.

To help you identify even more birds in Ohio, I have added 12 new species and 153 new color photographs. All of the range maps have been meticulously reviewed, and many updates have been made to reflect the ever-changing movements of the birds.

Everyone's favorite section, "Stan's Notes," has been expanded to include even more natural history information. "Compare" sections have been updated to help ensure that you correctly identify your bird, and additional feeder information has been added to help with bird feeding. I hope you will enjoy this great new edition as you continue to learn about and appreciate our Ohio birds!

WHY WATCH BIRDS IN OHIO?

Millions of people have discovered bird feeding. It's a simple and enjoyable way to bring the beauty of birds closer to your home. Watching birds at your feeder and listening to them often leads to a lifetime pursuit of bird identification. The *Birds of Ohio Field Guide* is for those who want to identify the common birds of Ohio.

There are over 1,100 species of birds found in North America. In Ohio alone there have been over 430 kinds of birds recorded through the years. These bird sightings were diligently recorded by hundreds of bird-watchers and became part of the official state record. From these records, I have chosen 124 of the most common birds of Ohio to include in this field guide.

Bird-watching, often called birding, is one of the most popular activities in America. Its outstanding appeal in Ohio is due, in part, to the state's unusually rich and abundant birdlife. Why are there so many birds? One reason is open space. Ohio is more than 44,000 square miles (114,400 sq. km), including parts of Lake Erie, making it the thirty-fourth-largest state. Despite its size, only about 12 million people call Ohio home. On average, that's only 272 people per square mile (104 per sq. km). Most are located in or around four major cities.

Open space is not the only reason there is such an abundance of birds. It's also the diversity of habitat. The state can be broken into several distinct habitats, each of which supports a different group of birds.

Ohio is divided into two regions: unglaciated and glaciated. An invisible line called the glacial boundary splits Ohio roughly down the middle and separates the eastern and western regions of the state.

The unglaciated region of Ohio is east and south of the glacial boundary. Here many small streams cut through deep valleys. The most extensive woodlands are also found in this portion of Ohio. Oak, hickory, beech, elm and maple trees in the southern forests are home to birds such as the Scarlet Tanager and Great Crested Flycatcher.

North and west of the glacial boundary is the glaciated region. Fewer hills are found here, but there is plenty of open farm-land with isolated woodlots and woodland edges. Here you can find prairie or open-land birds such as the Horned Lark.

Bordering northern Ohio is Lake Erie, one of the Great Lakes. This large freshwater lake is home to many species of birds such as the Herring Gull and Ring-billed Gull. The state's southern border is defined by the Ohio River. The cool, flowing water and shade-producing tall trees lining the riverbanks make this area a great place for birds. Green Herons can be seen stalking the wetlands in search of small fish, insects and small amphibians.

Besides the varying habitat, Ohio is well known for its weather. From the snowy winters in the northeastern part of the state to the steamy summers in southern Ohio, there are birds to watch in every season. Whether witnessing a migration of hawks in fall or welcoming back hummingbirds in spring, there is variety and excitement in birding as each season turns to the next.

OBSERVATION STRATEGIES: TIPS FOR IDENTIFYING BIRDS

Identifying birds isn't as difficult as you might think. By simply following a few basic strategies, you can increase your chances of successfully identifying most birds that you see. One of the first and easiest things to do when you see a new bird is to note its **color**. This field guide is organized by color, so simply turn to the right color section to find it.

Next, note the **size of the bird.** A strategy to quickly estimate size is to compare different birds. Pick a small, a medium and a large bird. Select an American Robin as the medium bird. Measured from bill tip to tail tip, a robin is 10 inches (25 cm). Now select two other birds, one smaller and one larger. Good choices are a House Sparrow, at about 6 inches (15 cm), and an American Crow, around 18 inches (45 cm). When you see a species you don't know, you can now quickly ask yourself, "Is it larger than a sparrow but smaller than a robin?" When you look in your field guide to identify your bird, you would check the species that are roughly 6–10 inches (15–25 cm). This will help to narrow your choices.

Next, note the **size, shape and color of the bill.** Is it long or short, thick or thin, pointed or blunt, curved or straight? Seed-eating birds, such as Northern Cardinals, have bills that are thick and strong enough to crack even the toughest seeds. Birds that sip nectar, such as Ruby-throated Hummingbirds, need long, thin bills to reach deep into flowers. Hawks and owls tear their prey with very sharp, curving bills. Sometimes, just noting the bill shape can help you decide whether the bird is a woodpecker, finch, grosbeak, blackbird or bird of prey.

Next, take a look around and note the **habitat** in which you see the bird. Is it wading in a marsh? Walking along a riverbank? Soaring in the sky? Is it perched high in the trees or hopping along the forest floor? Because of diet and habitat preferences, you'll often see robins hopping on the ground but not usually eating seeds at a feeder. Or you'll see a Blue Jay sitting on a tree branch but not climbing headfirst down the trunk, like a White-breasted Nuthatch would.

Noticing **what the bird is eating** will give you another clue to help you identify the species. Feeding is a big part of any bird's life. Fully one-third of all bird activity revolves around search-ing for food, catching prey and eating. While birds don't always follow all the rules of their diet, you can make some general assumptions. Northern Flickers, for instance, feed on ants and other insects, so you wouldn't expect to see them visiting a seed feeder. Other birds, such as Barn and Tree Swallows, eat flying insects and spend hours swooping and diving to catch a meal.

Sometimes you can identify a bird by **the way it perches.** Body posture can help you differentiate between an American Crow and a Red-tailed Hawk, for example. Crows lean forward over their feet on a branch, while hawks perch in a vertical position. Consider posture the next time you see an unidentified large bird in a tree.

Birds in flight are harder to identify, but noting the **wing size and shape** will help. Wing size is in direct proportion to body size, weight and type of flight. Wing shape determines whether the bird flies fast and with precision, or slowly and less precisely. Barn Swallows, for instance, have short, pointed wings that slice through the air, enabling swift, accurate flight. Turkey Vultures have long, broad wings for soaring on warm updrafts. House Finches have short, rounded wings, helping them to flit through thick tangles of branches.

Some bird species have a unique **pattern of flight** that can help in identification. American Goldfinches fly in a distinctive undulating pattern that makes it look like they're riding a roller coaster.

While it's not easy to make all of these observations in the short time you often have to watch a "mystery" bird, practicing these identification methods will greatly expand your birding skills. To further improve your skills, seek the guidance of a more experienced birder who can answer your questions on the spot.

BIRD BASICS

It's easier to identify birds and communicate about them if you know the names of the different parts of a bird. For instance, it's more effective to use the word "crest" to indicate the set of extra-long feathers on top of a Northern Cardinal's head than to try to describe it.

The following illustration points out the basic parts of a bird. Because it is a composite of many birds, it shouldn't be confused with any actual bird.

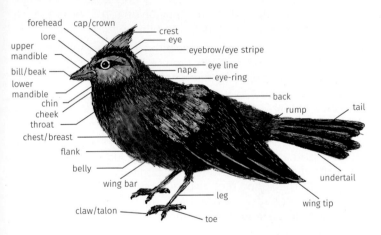

Bird Color Variables

No other animal has a color palette like a bird's. Brilliant blues, lemon yellows, showy reds and iridescent greens are common in the bird world. In general, male birds are more colorful than their female counterparts. This helps males attract a mate, essentially saying, "Hey, look at me!" Color calls attention to a male's health as well. The better the condition of his feathers, the better his food source, territory and potential for mating.

When male and female birds of the same species don't look like each other, they are called sexually dimorphic, meaning "two forms." Dimorphic females often have a nondescript, dull color, as seen in Indigo Buntings. Muted tones not only help females hide during the weeks of motionless incubation but also draw less attention to them when they're out feeding or taking a break from the rigors of raising the young.

The males and females of some species, such as the Downy Woodpecker, Blue Jay and Bald Eagle, look nearly identical. In woodpeckers, they are differentiated by only a red (sometimes yellow or black) mark; this mark may be on top of the head, on the face or nape, or just behind the bill.

During the first year, juvenile birds often look like their mothers. Since brightly colored feathers are used mainly for attracting a mate, young non-breeding males don't have a need for colorful plumage. It's not until the first spring molt (or several years later, depending on the species) that young males obtain their breeding colors.

Both breeding and winter plumages are the result of molting. Molting is the process of dropping old, worn feathers and replacing them with new ones. All birds molt, typically twice a year, with the spring molt usually occurring in late winter. At this time, most birds produce their brighter breeding plumage, which lasts throughout the summer.

Winter plumage is the result of the late-summer molt, which serves a couple of important functions. First, it adds feathers for warmth in the coming winter season. Second, in some species it produces feathers that tend to be drab in color, which helps to camouflage the birds and hide them from predators. The winter plumage of the male American Goldfinch, for example, is olive brown, unlike its canary-yellow breeding color during summer. Luckily for us, some birds, such as the male Northern Cardinal, retain their bright summer colors all year long.

Bird Nests

Bird nests are a true feat of engineering. Imagine constructing a home that's strong enough to weather storms, large enough to hold your entire family, insulated enough to shelter them from cold and heat, and waterproof enough to keep out rain. Think about building it without blueprints or directions and using mainly your feet. Birds do this!

Before building, birds must select an appropriate site. In some species, such as the House Wren, the male picks out several potential sites and assembles small twigs in each. The "extra" nests, called dummy nests, discourage other birds from using any nearby cavities for their nests. The male takes the female around and shows her the choices. After choosing her favorite, she finishes the construction.

In other species, such as the Baltimore Oriole, the female selects the site and builds the nest, while the male offers an occasional suggestion. Each bird species has its own nest-building routine that is strictly followed.

As you can see in these illustrations, birds build a wide variety of nest types.

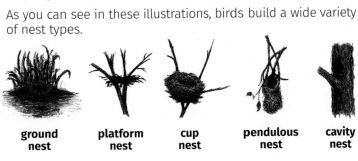

| ground nest | platform nest | cup nest | pendulous nest | cavity nest |

Nesting material often consists of natural items found in the immediate area. Most nests consist of plant fibers (such as bark from grapevines), sticks, mud, dried grass, feathers, fur, or soft, fuzzy tufts from thistle. Some birds, including Ruby-throated Hummingbirds, use spiderwebs to glue nest materials together.

Transportation of nesting material is limited to the amount a bird can hold or carry. Birds must make many trips afield to gather enough material to complete a nest. Most nests take four days or more, and hundreds, if not thousands, of trips to build.

A **ground nest** can be a mound of vegetation on the ground or in the water. It can also be just a simple, shallow depression scraped out in earth, stones or sand. Killdeer and Horned Larks scrape out ground nests without adding any nesting material.

The **platform nest** represents a much more complex type of construction. Typically built with twigs or sticks and branches, this nest forms a platform and has a depression in the center to nestle the eggs. Platform nests can be in trees; on balconies, cliffs, bridges, or man-made platforms; and even in flowerpots. They often provide space for the adventurous young and function as a landing platform for the parents.

Mourning Doves and herons don't anchor their platform nests to trees, so these can tumble from branches during high winds and storms. Hawks, eagles, ospreys and other birds construct sturdier platform nests with large sticks and branches.

Other platform nests are constructed on the ground with mud, grass and other vegetation from the area. Many waterfowl build platform nests on the ground near or in water. A **floating platform nest** moves with the water level, preventing the nest, eggs and birds from being flooded.

Three-quarters of all songbirds construct a **cup nest,** which is a modified platform nest. The supporting platform is built first and attached firmly to a tree, shrub, or rock ledge or the ground. Next, the sides are constructed with grass, small twigs, bark or leaves, which are woven together and often glued with mud for added strength. The inner cup can be lined with down feathers, animal fur or hair, or soft plant materials and is contoured last.

The **pendulous nest** is an unusual nest that looks like a sock hanging from a branch. Attached to the end of small branches of trees, this unique nest is inaccessible to most predators and often waves wildly in a breeze.

Woven tightly with plant fibers, the pendulous nest is strong and watertight and takes up to a week to build. A small opening at the top or on the side allows parents access to the grass-lined interior. More commonly used by tropical birds, this complex nest has also been mastered by orioles and kinglets. It must be one heck of a ride to be inside one of these nests during a windy spring thunderstorm!

The **cavity nest** is used by many species of birds, most notably woodpeckers and Eastern Bluebirds. A cavity nest is often excavated from a branch or tree trunk and offers shelter from storms, sun, cold and predators. A small entrance hole in a tree can lead to a nest chamber that is up to a safe 10 inches (25 cm) deep.

Typically made by woodpeckers, cavity nests are usually used only once by the builder. Nest cavities can be used for many subsequent years by such inhabitants as Tree Swallows, mergansers and bluebirds. Kingfishers, on the other hand, can dig a tunnel up to 4 feet (1 m) long in a riverbank. The nest chamber at the end of the tunnel is already well insulated, so it's usually only sparsely lined.

One of the most clever of all nests is the **no nest,** or daycare nest. Parasitic birds, such as Brown-headed Cowbirds, don't build their own nests. Instead, the egg-laden female searches out the nest of another bird and sneaks in to lay an egg while the host mother isn't looking.

A mother cowbird wastes no energy building a nest only to have it raided by a predator. Laying her eggs in the nests of other birds transfers the responsibility of raising her young to the host. When she lays her eggs in several nests, the chances increase that at least one of her babies will live to maturity.

Who Builds the Nest?

Generally, the female bird constructs the nest. She gathers the materials and does the building, with an occasional visit from her mate to check on progress. In some species, both parents contribute equally to nest building. The male may forage for sticks, grass or mud, but it is the female that often fashions the nest. Only rarely does a male build a nest by himself.

Fledging

Fledging is the time between hatching and flight, or leaving the nest. Some species of birds are **precocial,** meaning they leave the nest within hours of hatching, though it may be weeks before they can fly. This is common in waterfowl and shorebirds.

Baby birds that hatch naked and blind need to stay in the nest for a few weeks (these birds are **altricial**). Baby birds that are still in the nest are **nestlings.** Until birds start to fly, they are called **fledglings.**

Why Birds Migrate

Why do so many species of birds migrate? The short answer is simple: food. Birds migrate to locations with abundant food, as it is easier to breed where there is food than where food is scarce. Scarlet Tanagers, for instance, are **complete migrators** that fly from the tropics of South America to nest in the forests of North America, where billions of newly hatched insects are available to feed to their young.

Other migrators, such as some birds of prey, migrate back to northern regions in spring. In these locations, they hunt mice, voles and other small rodents that are beginning to breed.

Complete migrators have a set time and pattern of migration. Every year at nearly the same time, they head to a specific wintering ground. Complete migrators may travel great distances, sometimes 15,000 miles (24,100 km) or more in one year.

Complete migration doesn't necessarily mean flying from Ohio to a tropical destination. Dark-eyed Juncos, for example, are complete migrators that move from the far reaches of Canada to spend the winter here in cold and snowy Ohio. This trip is still considered complete migration.

Complete migrators have many interesting aspects. In spring, males often leave a few weeks before the females, arriving early to scope out possibilities for nesting sites and food sources, and to begin to defend territories. The females arrive several weeks later. In many species, the females and their young leave earlier in the fall, often up to four weeks before the adult males.

Other species, such as the American Goldfinch, are **partial migrators**. These birds usually wait until their food supplies dwindle before flying south. Unlike complete migrators, partial migrators move only far enough south, or sometimes east and west, to find abundant food. In some years it might be only a few hundred miles, while in other years it can be as much as a thousand. This kind of migration, dependent on weather and the availability of food, is sometimes called seasonal movement.

Unlike the predictable complete migrators or partial migrators, **irruptive migrators** can move every third to fifth year or, in some cases, in consecutive years. These migrations are triggered when times are tough and food is scarce. Red-breasted Nuthatches are irruptive migrators. They leave their normal northern range in search of more food or in response to overpopulation.

Many other birds don't migrate at all. Black-capped Chickadees, for example, are **non-migrators** that remain in their habitat all year long and just move around as necessary to find food.

How Birds Migrate

One of the many secrets of migration is fat. While most people are fighting the ongoing battle of the bulge, birds intentionally gorge themselves to gain as much fat as possible without losing the ability to fly. Fat provides the greatest amount of energy per unit of weight. In the same way that your car needs gas, birds are propelled by fat and stall without it.

During long migratory flights, fat deposits are used up quickly, and birds need to stop to refuel. This is when backyard bird feeding stations and undeveloped, natural spaces around our towns and cities are especially important. Some birds require up to 2–3 days of constant feeding to build their fat reserves before continuing their seasonal trip.

Many birds, such as most eagles, hawks, ospreys, falcons and vultures, migrate during the day. Larger birds can hold more body fat, go longer without eating and take longer to migrate. These birds glide along on rising columns of warm air, called thermals, that hold them aloft while they slowly make their way north or south. They generally rest at night and hunt early in the morning before the sun has a chance to warm the land and create good soaring conditions. Daytime migrators use a combination of landforms, rivers, and the rising and setting sun to guide them in the right direction.

The majority of small birds, called **passerines,** migrate at night. Studies show that some use the stars to navigate. Others use the setting sun, and still others, such as pigeons, use Earth's magnetic field to guide them north or south.

While flying at night may not seem like a good idea, it's actually safer. First, there are fewer avian predators hunting for birds at night. Second, night travel allows time during the day to find food in unfamiliar surroundings. Third, wind patterns at night tend to be flat, or laminar. Flat winds don't have the turbulence of daytime winds and can help push the smaller birds along.

HOW TO USE THIS GUIDE

To help you quickly and easily identify birds, this field guide is organized by color. Refer to the color key on the first page, note the color of the bird, and turn to that section. For example, the male Rose-breasted Grosbeak is black-and-white with a red patch on his chest. Because the bird is mostly black-and-white, it will be found in the black-and-white section.

Each color section is also arranged by size, generally with the smaller birds first. Sections may also incorporate the average size in a range, which in some cases reflects size differences between male and female birds. Flip through the pages in the color section to find the bird. If you already know the name of the bird, check the index for the page number.

In some species, the male and female are very different in color. In others, the breeding and winter plumage colors differ. These species will have an inset photograph with a page reference and will be found in two color sections.

You will find a variety of information in the bird description sections. To learn more, turn to the sample on pp. 20–21.

Range Maps

Range maps are included for each bird. Colored areas indicate where the bird is frequently found. The colors represent the presence of a species during a specific season, not the density, or amount, of birds in the area. Green is used for summer, blue for winter, red for year-round and yellow for migration.

While every effort has been made to depict accurate ranges, these are constantly in flux due to a variety of factors. Changing weather, habitat, species abundance and availability of vital resources, such as food and water, can affect the migration and movement of local populations, causing birds to be found in areas that are atypical for the species. So please use the maps as intended—as general guides only.

female
p. 107

male

Common Name

—Range Map   *Scientific name*   **Color Indicator—**

YEAR-ROUND
SUMMER
MIGRATION
WINTER

Size: measurement is from head to tip of tail; wingspan may be listed as well

Male: brief description of the male bird; may include breeding, winter or other plumages

Female: brief description of the female bird, which is sometimes different from the male

Juvenile: brief description of the juvenile bird, which often looks like the adult female

Nest: kind of nest the bird builds to raise its young; who builds it; number of broods per year

Eggs: number of eggs you might expect to see in a nest; color and marking

Incubation: average days the parents spend incubating the eggs; who does the incubation

Fledging: average days the young spend in the nest after hatching but before they leave the nest; who does the most "childcare" and feeding

Migration: type of migrator: complete (seasonal, consistent), partial (seasonal, destination varies), irruptive (unpredictable, depends on the food supply) or non-migrator

Food: what the bird eats most of the time (e.g., seeds, insects, fruit, nectar, small mammals, fish) and whether it typically comes to a bird feeder

Compare: notes about other birds that look similar and the pages on which they can be found; may include extra information to aid in identification

Stan's Notes: Interesting natural history information. This could be something to look or listen for or something to help positively identify the bird. Also includes remarkable features.

female
p. 125

male

Eastern Towhee
Pipilo erythrophthalmus

YEAR-ROUND
SUMMER

Size:	7–8" (18–20 cm)
Male:	Mostly black with rusty-brown sides and a white belly. Long black tail with a white tip. Short, stout, pointed bill and rich-red eyes. White wing patches flash in flight.
Female:	similar to male but brown instead of black
Juvenile:	light brown with a heavily streaked head, chest and belly. Long, dark tail with a white tip
Nest:	cup; female builds; 2 broods per year
Eggs:	3–4; cream white with brown markings
Incubation:	12–13 days; female incubates
Fledging:	10–12 days; male and female feed the young
Migration:	non-migrator to partial, to southern Ohio and southern states
Food:	insects, seeds, fruit; visits ground feeders
Compare:	The American Robin (p. 231) lacks the white belly. The Gray Catbird (p. 229) lacks the black head and rusty sides. The Common Grackle (p. 31) lacks a white belly and has a long, thin bill. The male Rose-breasted Grosbeak (p. 49) has a rosy patch on its chest.

Stan's Notes: Named for its distinctive "tow-hee" call (given by both sexes) but known mostly for its other characteristic call, which sounds like "drink-your-tea!" Will hop backward with both feet (bilateral scratching), raking up leaf litter to locate insects and seeds. Male feeds the young most of the time.

female
p. 127

male

Brown-headed Cowbird
Molothrus ater

YEAR-ROUND

Size: 7½" (19 cm)

Male: glossy black with a chocolate-brown head; a pointed, sharp, gray bill; and dark eyes

Female: dull brown with a pointed, sharp, gray bill

Juvenile: similar to female but with dull-gray plumage and a streaked chest

Nest: no nest; lays eggs in the nests of other birds

Eggs: 5–7; white with brown markings

Incubation: 10–13 days; host birds incubate the eggs

Fledging: 10–11 days; host birds feed the young

Migration: non-migrator in Ohio; moves around to find food

Food: insects, seeds; will come to seed feeders

Compare: The male Red-winged Blackbird (p. 29) is slightly larger and has red-and-yellow patches on its upper wings. The Common Grackle (p. 31) has a long tail and lacks the brown head. The European Starling (p. 27) has a shorter tail.

Stan's Notes: Cowbirds are members of the blackbird family. Known as brood parasites, Brown-headed Cowbirds are the only parasitic birds in Ohio. Brood parasites lay their eggs in the nests of other birds, leaving the host birds to raise their young. Cowbirds are known to have laid their eggs in the nests of over 200 species of birds. While some birds reject cowbird eggs, most incubate them and raise the young, even to the exclusion of their own. Look for warblers and other birds feeding young birds twice their own size. Named "Cowbird" for its habit of following bison and cattle herds to feed on insects flushed up by the animals.

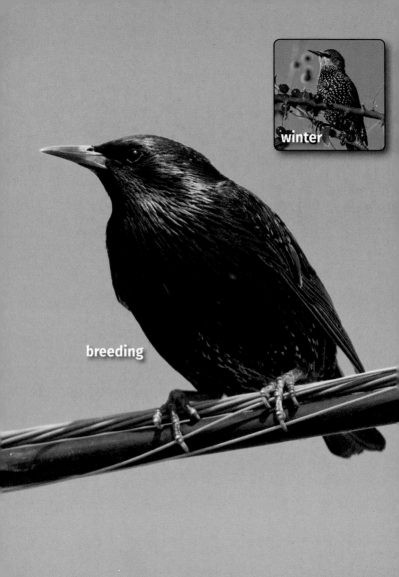

winter

breeding

European Starling
Sturnus vulgaris

YEAR-ROUND

Size: 7½" (19 cm)

Male: Glittering, iridescent purplish black in spring and summer; duller and speckled with white in fall and winter. Long, pointed, yellow bill in spring; gray in fall. Pointed wings. Short tail.

Female: same as male

Juvenile: similar to adults, with grayish-brown plumage and a streaked chest

Nest: cavity; male and female line the cavity; 2 broods per year

Eggs: 4–6; bluish with brown markings

Incubation: 12–14 days; female and male incubate

Fledging: 18–20 days; female and male feed the young

Migration: non-migrator to partial; some will move to southern states

Food: insects, seeds, fruit; visits seed or suet feeders

Compare: The Common Grackle (p. 31) has a long tail. The male Brown-headed Cowbird (p. 25) has a brown head. Look for the shiny, dark feathers to help identify the European Starling.

Stan's Notes: One of our most numerous songbirds. Mimics the songs of up to 20 bird species and imitates sounds, including the human voice. Jaws are more powerful when opening than when closing, enabling the bird to pry open crevices to find insects. Often displaces woodpeckers, chickadees and other cavity-nesting birds. Large families gather with blackbirds in the fall. Not a native bird; 100 starlings were introduced to New York City in 1890–91 from Europe. Bill changes color with the seasons in spring and fall.

female
p. 139

male

Red-winged Blackbird
Agelaius phoeniceus

YEAR-ROUND

Size: 8½" (21.5 cm)

Male: Jet black with red-and-yellow patches (epaulets) on upper wings. Pointed black bill.

Female: heavily streaked brown with a pointed brown bill and white eyebrows

Juvenile: same as female

Nest: cup; female builds; 2–3 broods per year

Eggs: 3–4; bluish green with brown markings

Incubation: 10–12 days; female incubates

Fledging: 11–14 days; female and male feed the young

Migration: non-migrator to partial; some will move to southern states, Mexico and Central America

Food: seeds, insects; visits seed and suet feeders

Compare: The male Brown-headed Cowbird (p. 25) is smaller and glossier and has a brown head. The bold red-and-yellow epaulets distinguish the male Red-winged from other blackbirds.

Stan's Notes: One of the most widespread and numerous birds in Ohio. Found around marshes, wetlands, lakes and rivers. It is a sure sign of spring when these birds return home. Flocks with as many as 10,000 birds have been reported. Males arrive before the females and sing to defend their territory. The male repeats his call from the top of a cattail while showing off his red-and-yellow shoulder patches. The female chooses a mate and often builds her nest over shallow water in a thick stand of cattails. The male can be aggressive when defending the nest. Red-winged Blackbirds feed mostly on seeds in spring and fall, and insects throughout the summer.

Common Grackle

Quiscalus quiscula

YEAR-ROUND

Size: 11–13" (28–33 cm)

Male: large, iridescent blackbird with bluish-black head; purplish-brown body; long black tail; long, thin bill; and bright-golden eyes

Female: similar to male but smaller and duller

Juvenile: similar to female

Nest: cup; female builds; 2 broods per year

Eggs: 4–5; greenish white with brown markings

Incubation: 13–14 days; female incubates

Fledging: 16–20 days; female and male feed the young

Migration: non-migrator to partial in Ohio; will move around the state in search of food

Food: fruit, seeds, insects; will come to seed and suet feeders

Compare: The European Starling (p. 27) is much smaller with a speckled appearance and a yellow bill during the breeding season. The male Red-winged Blackbird (p. 29) has bright red-and-yellow shoulder patches (epaulets).

Stan's Notes: Usually nests in small colonies of up to 75 pairs but travels with other blackbird species in large flocks. Known to feed in farm fields. The common name is derived from the Latin word *gracula*, meaning "jackdaw," another species of bird and a term that can refer to any bird in the *Quiscalus* genus. The male holds his tail in a deep V shape during flight. The flight pattern is usually level, as opposed to an undulating movement. Unlike most birds, it has larger muscles for opening its mouth than for closing it, enabling it to pry crevices apart to find hidden insects.

American Coot
Fulica americana

SUMMER MIGRATION

Size: 13–16" (33–41 cm)

Male: Gray to black waterbird. Duck-like white bill with a dark band near the tip and a small red patch near the eyes. Small white patch near base of tail. Green legs and feet. Red eyes.

Female: same as male

Juvenile: much paler than adults, with a gray bill

Nest: floating platform; female and male construct; 1 brood per year

Eggs: 9–12; pinkish buff with brown markings

Incubation: 21–25 days; female and male incubate

Fledging: 49–52 days; female and male feed the young

Migration: complete, to southern states, Mexico and Central America

Food: insects, aquatic plants

Compare: Smaller than most waterfowl. This is the only black duck-like bird with a white bill.

Stan's Notes: Usually seen in large flocks on open water. Not a duck, as it has large lobed toes instead of webbed feet. An excellent diver and swimmer, bobbing its head as it swims. A favorite food of Bald Eagles. It is not often seen in flight, unless it's trying to escape from an eagle. To take off, it scrambles across the surface of the water, flapping its wings. Gives a unique series of creaks, groans and clicks. Anchors its floating platform nest to vegetation. Huge flocks with as many as 1,000 birds gather for migration. Migrates at night. The common name "Coot" comes from the Middle English word *coote*, which was used to describe various waterfowl. Also called Mud Hen.

in flight

American Crow
Corvus brachyrhynchos

YEAR-ROUND

Size: 18" (45 cm)

Male: All-black bird with black bill, legs and feet. Can have a purple sheen in direct sunlight.

Female: same as male

Juvenile: same as adults

Nest: platform; female builds; 1 brood per year

Eggs: 4–6; bluish to olive with brown markings

Incubation: 18 days; female incubates

Fledging: 28–35 days; female and male feed the young

Migration: non-migrator to partial; some will move into cities during the winter

Food: fruit, insects, mammals, fish, carrion; comes to seed and suet feeders

Compare: The Common Raven (p. 37) has a larger bill; shaggy throat feathers; a deep, raspy call; and a wedged tail, as seen in flight. Look for the glossy black plumage and squared tail to help identify the American Crow.

Stan's Notes: A familiar bird, found in all habitats. Imitates other birds and human voices. One of the smartest of all birds and very social, often entertaining itself by provoking chases with other birds. Eats roadkill but is rarely hit by vehicles. Can live as long as 20 years. Often reuses its nest every year if it's not taken over by a Great Horned Owl. Unmated birds, known as helpers, help to raise the young. Extended families roost together at night, dispersing daily to hunt. Cannot soar on thermals; flaps constantly and glides downward. Gathers in huge communal flocks of up to 10,000 birds in winter.

in flight

Common Raven
Corvus corax

YEAR-ROUND

Size: 22–27" (56–69 cm)

Male: Large all-black bird with a shaggy beard of feathers on the throat and a large black bill. Large wedge-shaped tail, best seen in flight.

Female: same as male

Juvenile: same as adults

Nest: platform; female and male construct; 1 brood per year

Eggs: 4–6; pale green with brown markings

Incubation: 18–21 days; female incubates

Fledging: 38–44 days; female and male feed the young

Migration: non-migrator to partial; will move around in search of food

Food: insects, fruit, small animals, carrion

Compare: The American Crow (p. 35) is smaller and lacks the shaggy throat feathers. The Raven glides on flat, outstretched wings, unlike the slight V-shaped wing pattern of the Crow. Listen for the Raven's deep, raspy call to distinguish it from the Crow's higher-pitched call.

Stan's Notes: Considered by some to be the smartest of all birds. Known for its aerial acrobatics and long, swooping dives. Sometimes scavenges with crows and gulls. A cooperative hunter that often communicates the location of a food source to other ravens. Until recently, it was rare in Ohio. Most start to breed at 3–4 years. Complex courtship includes grabbing bills, preening each other and cooing. Long-term pair bond. Uses the same nest site for many years.

soaring

juvenile

Black Vulture
Coragyps atratus

YEAR-ROUND

Size: 25–28" (63–71 cm); up to 5¼' wingspan

Male: Black with dark-gray head and legs. Short tail. In flight, all black with light-gray wing tips.

Female: same as male

Juvenile: similar to adults

Nest: no nest, on a stump or on the ground, or takes an abandoned nest; 1 brood per year

Eggs: 1–3; light green with dark markings

Incubation: 37–45 days; female and male incubate

Fledging: 75–80 days; female and male feed the young

Migration: non-migrator; moves around in winter to find food

Food: carrion; occasionally will capture small live mammals

Compare: Slightly smaller than the Turkey Vulture (p. 41) and lacking its bright-red head. The Turkey Vulture has two-toned wings with a black leading edge and light-gray trailing edge. The Black Vulture also has shorter, gray-tipped wings and a shorter tail.

Stan's Notes: Also called Black Buzzard. A more gregarious bird than the Turkey Vulture. In flight, the Black Vulture holds its wings straight out to its sides, unlike the Turkey Vulture, which holds its wings in a V pattern. More aggressive while feeding but less skilled at finding carrion than the Turkey Vulture; it is thought the Black Vulture's sense of smell is less developed. Families stay together up to a year. Often nests and roosts with other Black Vultures. If startled, especially at the nest, it regurgitates with power and accuracy.

soaring

juvenile

Turkey Vulture
Cathartes aura

Size: 26–32" (66–81 cm); up to 6' wingspan

Male: Large and black with a naked red head and legs. In flight, wings are two-toned with a black leading edge and a gray trailing edge. Wing tips end in finger-like projections. Tail is long and squared. Ivory bill.

Female: same as male but slightly smaller

Juvenile: similar to adults, with a gray to blackish head and bill

Nest: no nest or minimal nest, on a cliff or in a cave, sometimes in a hollow tree; 1 brood per year

Eggs: 1–3; white with brown markings

Incubation: 38–41 days; female and male incubate

Fledging: 66–88 days; female and male feed the young

Migration: non-migrator to complete, to southern states, Mexico, and Central and South America

Food: carrion; parents regurgitate to feed the young

Compare: The Bald Eagle (p. 73) is much larger and lacks two-toned wings. Look for the obvious naked red head to identify the Turkey Vulture.

Stan's Notes: The naked head reduces the risk of feather fouling (picking up diseases) from contact with carcasses. It has a strong bill for tearing apart flesh. Unlike hawks and eagles, it has weak feet more suited for walking than grasping. One of the few birds with a developed sense of smell. Mostly mute, making only grunts and groans. Holds its wings in an upright V shape in flight. Teeters from wing tip to wing tip as it soars and hovers. Seen in trees with wings outstretched, sunning itself and drying after a rain.

in flight

juvenile

crests

drying

Double-crested Cormorant
Phalacrocorax auritus

YEAR-ROUND
MIGRATION

Size: 31–35" (79–89 cm); up to 4⅓' wingspan

Male: large black waterbird with unusual blue-teal eyes; a long, snake-like neck; and a large gray bill with yellow at the base and a hooked tip

Female: same as male

Juvenile: lighter brown with a grayish chest and neck

Nest: platform; male and female construct; 1 brood per year

Eggs: 3–4; bluish white without markings

Incubation: 25–29 days; female and male incubate

Fledging: 37–42 days; male and female feed the young

Migration: complete, to southern states, Mexico and Central America; winters in Ohio along Lake Erie

Food: small fish, aquatic insects

Compare: The Turkey Vulture (p. 41) also spreads out its wings to dry in the sun, but it has a naked red head. The American Coot (p. 33) has a duck-like white bill. Look for the long, snake-like neck and large, hooked bill to help identify the Cormorant.

Stan's Notes: Flies in a large V or a line. Usually roosts in large colonies in trees close to water. Swims underwater to catch fish, holding its wings at its sides. Lacks the oil gland that keeps feathers from becoming waterlogged. To dry off, it strikes an upright pose with wings outstretched, facing the sun. Gives grunts, pops and groans. Named "Double-crested" for the crests on its head, which are not often seen. "Cormorant" is a contraction from *corvus marinus*, meaning "crow" or "raven," and "of the sea."

male

female

Black-and-white Warbler
Mniotilta varia

SUMMER

Size: 5" (13 cm)

Male: Small with zebra-like striping and a black-and-white striped crown. Black cheek patch and chin. White belly.

Female: duller than male and lacks a black cheek patch and chin

Juvenile: similar to female

Nest: cup; female builds; 1 brood per year

Eggs: 4–5; white with brown markings

Incubation: 10–11 days; female incubates

Fledging: 9–12 days; female and male feed the young

Migration: complete, to Florida, Mexico, and Central and South America

Food: insects

Compare: Climbs down tree trunks headfirst, like the White-breasted Nuthatch (p. 213) and Red-breasted Nuthatch (p. 207). Look for a small black-and-white bird climbing down trees to identify the Black-and-white Warbler.

Stan's Notes: This is the only warbler species that moves down tree trunks headfirst. Look for it searching for insect eggs in the bark of large trees. Its song sounds like a slowly turning, squeaky wheel going around and around. Female performs a distraction dance to draw predators away from the nest. Constructs its nest on the ground, concealing it under dead leaves or at the base of a tree. Found in a variety of habitats. Can be one of the more common warbler species during migration in both spring and fall.

male

female

Downy Woodpecker
Dryobates pubescens

YEAR-ROUND

Size:	6" (15 cm)
Male:	Small woodpecker with a white belly and black-and-white spotted wings. Red mark on the back of the head and a white stripe down the back. Short black bill.
Female:	same as male but lacks the red mark
Juvenile:	same as female, some with a red mark near the forehead
Nest:	cavity with a round entrance hole; male and female excavate; 1 brood per year
Eggs:	3–5; white without markings
Incubation:	11–12 days; female incubates during the day, male incubates at night
Fledging:	20–25 days; male and female feed the young
Migration:	non-migrator
Food:	insects, seeds; visits suet and seed feeders
Compare:	The Hairy Woodpecker (p. 53) is larger. Look for the Downy's shorter, thinner bill.

Stan's Notes: Abundant and widespread where trees are present. This is perhaps the most common woodpecker in the U.S. Stiff tail feathers help to brace it like a tripod as it clings to a tree. Like other woodpeckers, it has a long, barbed tongue to pull insects from tiny places. Mates drum on branches or hollow logs to announce territory, which is rarely larger than 5 acres (2 ha). Repeats a high-pitched "peek-peek" call. Nest cavity is wider at the bottom than at the top and is lined with fallen wood chips. Male performs most of the brooding. During winter, it will roost in a cavity. Undulates in flight.

female
p. 133

male

SUMMER
MIGRATION

Rose-breasted Grosbeak
Pheucticus ludovicianus

Size: 7–8" (18–20 cm)

Male: Plump black-and-white bird with a large triangular, rose-colored patch on the breast. Wing linings are rose red. Large ivory bill.

Female: heavily streaked with obvious white eyebrows and orange to yellow wing linings

Juvenile: similar to female

Nest: cup; female and male construct; 1–2 broods per year

Eggs: 3–5; blue green with brown markings

Incubation: 13–14 days; female and male incubate

Fledging: 9–12 days; female and male feed the young

Migration: complete, to Mexico, Central America and South America

Food: insects, seeds, fruit; comes to seed feeders

Compare: Male is very distinctive, with no look-alikes. Look for the rose breast patch to identify.

Stan's Notes: Seen in small groups. Prefers a mature deciduous forest for nesting. Both sexes sing, but the male sings much louder and clearer. Sings a rich, robin-like song with a chip note in the tune. "Grosbeak" refers to the thick, strong bill, which is used to crush seeds. The rose patch varies in size and shape in each male. Males have white wing patches that flash during flight. Males arrive at the breeding grounds a few days before the females. Several males will come to seed feeders together in spring. When the females arrive, males become territorial and reduce their feeder visits. After fledging, young grosbeaks visit feeders with the adults. Makes short flights from tree to tree with rapid wingbeats.

male

female

Yellow-bellied Sapsucker

Sphyrapicus varius

SUMMER
MIGRATION
WINTER

Size: 8–9" (20–23 cm)

Male: Checkered back with a red forehead, crown and chin. Yellow to tan on the chest and belly. White wing patches are seen flashing in flight.

Female: similar to male but with a white chin

Juvenile: similar to female but dull brown and lacks red markings

Nest: cavity; female and male excavate, often in a live tree; 1 brood per year

Eggs: 5–6; white without markings

Incubation: 12–13 days; female incubates during the day, male incubates at night

Fledging: 25–29 days; female and male feed the young

Migration: complete, to southern Ohio, southern states, Mexico and Central America

Food: insects, tree sap; comes to suet feeders

Compare: The Red-headed Woodpecker (p. 55) has an all-red head. Look for the red chin and crown to identify the male Sapsucker, and the white chin and red crown to identify the female.

Stan's Notes: Found in small woods, forests, and suburban and rural areas. Drills rows of holes in trees to bleed the sap. Oozing sap attracts bugs, which it also eats. Defends its sapping sites from other birds that try to drink from the taps. Does not suck sap; rather, it laps the sticky liquid with its long, bristly tongue. A quiet bird, it makes few vocalizations but will meow like a cat. Drums on hollow branches, but unlike other woodpeckers, its rhythm is irregular. Makes short undulating flights with rapid wingbeats.

male

female

Hairy Woodpecker
Leuconotopicus villosus

YEAR-ROUND

Size:	9" (23 cm)
Male:	Black-and-white woodpecker with a white belly. Black wings with rows of white spots. White stripe down the back. Long black bill. Red mark on the back of the head.
Female:	same as male but lacks the red mark
Juvenile:	grayer version of the female
Nest:	cavity with an oval entrance hole; female and male excavate; 1 brood per year
Eggs:	3–6; white without markings
Incubation:	11–15 days; female incubates during the day, male incubates at night
Fledging:	28–30 days; male and female feed the young
Migration:	non-migrator
Food:	insects, nuts, seeds; will come to suet and seed feeders
Compare:	Much larger than the Downy Woodpecker (p. 47) and has a much longer bill, nearly equal to the width of its head.

Stan's Notes: A common bird in wooded backyards. Announces its arrival with a sharp chirp before landing on feeders. Responsible for eating many destructive forest insects. Uses its barbed tongue to extract insects from trees. Tiny, bristle-like feathers at the base of the bill protect the nostrils from wood dust. Drums on hollow logs, branches or stovepipes in spring to announce territory. Often prefers to excavate nest cavities in live aspen trees. Excavates a larger, more-oval-shaped entrance than the round entrance hole of the Downy Woodpecker. Makes short flights from tree to tree.

juvenile

Red-headed Woodpecker
Melanerpes erythrocephalus

YEAR-ROUND

Size: 9" (23 cm)

Male: All-red head with a solid black back. Black wings with large white wing patches seen flashing in flight. Black tail. White chest, belly and rump. Gray legs and bill.

Female: same as male

Juvenile: grayish-brown head and white chest

Nest: cavity; male excavates with some help from the female; 1 brood per year

Eggs: 4–5; white without markings

Incubation: 12–13 days; female and male incubate

Fledging: 27–30 days; female and male feed the young

Migration: non-migrator; will move to areas with an abundant supply of nuts

Food: insects, nuts, fruit; visits suet and seed feeders

Compare: No other woodpecker in Ohio has an all-red head. The Pileated Woodpecker (p. 67) is the only other woodpecker with a solid black back, but it has a partial red head.

Stan's Notes: One of the few non-dimorphic woodpeckers, with males and females that look alike. Bill is strong enough to excavate a nest cavity only in soft, dead trees. Prefers open woodlands or woodland edges with many dead or rotting branches. Nests later than its close relative, the Red-bellied Woodpecker, and will often take its cavity, if vacant. Unlike other woodpeckers, which use nest cavities just once briefly, it may use the same cavity for several years in a row. Often perches on top of dead snags. Stores acorns and other nuts. Gives a shrill, hoarse "churr" call.

male

female

Red-bellied Woodpecker
Melanerpes carolinus

YEAR-ROUND

Size: 9–9½" (23–24 cm)

Male: Black-and-white "zebra-backed" woodpecker with a white rump. Red crown extends down the nape of the neck. Tan chest. Pale-red tinge on the belly, often hard to see.

Female: same as male but with a light-gray crown and a red nape

Juvenile: gray version of adults; lacks a red crown and red nape

Nest: cavity; female and male excavate; 1 brood per year

Eggs: 4–5; white without markings

Incubation: 12–14 days; female incubates during the day, male incubates at night

Fledging: 24–27 days; female and male feed the young

Migration: non-migrator; moves around to find food

Food: insects, nuts, fruit; visits suet and seed feeders

Compare: Similar to the Northern Flicker (p. 155) and Yellow-bellied Sapsucker (p. 51). Look for the zebra-striped back to help identify the Red-bellied Woodpecker.

Stan's Notes: Likes shady woodlands, forest edges and backyards. Digs holes in rotten wood to find spiders, centipedes, beetles and more. Hammers acorns and berries into crevices of trees for winter food. Returns to the same tree to excavate a new nest below that of the previous year. Undulating flight with rapid wingbeats. Gives a loud "querrr" call and a low "chug-chug-chug." Named for the pale red tinge on its belly. Expanding its range all over the country.

female p. 169

male

Lesser Scaup
Aythya affinis

MIGRATION
WINTER

Size: 16–17" (40–43 cm)

Male: Appears mostly black with bold white sides and a gray back. Chest and head look nearly black, but head appears purple with green highlights in direct sun. Bright-yellow eyes.

Female: overall brown with a dull-white patch at the base of a light-gray bill; yellow eyes

Juvenile: same as female

Nest: ground; female builds; 1 brood per year

Eggs: 8–14; olive buff without markings

Incubation: 22–28 days; female incubates

Fledging: 45–50 days; female teaches the young to feed

Migration: complete to northern Ohio along Lake Erie; moves around to find open water and food

Food: aquatic plants and insects

Compare: The male Common Goldeneye (p. 65) has a white chest. The male Blue-winged Teal (p. 165) is slightly smaller, with a white crescent on its bill. The white sides and gray back help identify the male Lesser Scaup.

Stan's Notes: A common diving duck. Often seen in large flocks on lakes and ponds. Submerges completely to feed on the bottom (unlike dabbling ducks, which tip forward to reach the bottom). Note the bold white stripe under the wings when in flight. The male leaves the female when she starts incubating eggs. Egg quantity (clutch size) increases with the female's age. Has an interesting babysitting arrangement: groups of young (crèches) are tended by one to three adult females.

male

female
p. 175

Hooded Merganser
Lophodytes cucullatus

YEAR-ROUND

Size: 16–19" (41–48 cm)

Male: Black and white with rust-brown sides. Crest "hood" raises to show a large white patch on each side of the head. Long, thin, black bill.

Female: brown and rust with ragged, rust-red "hair" and a long, thin, brown bill

Juvenile: similar to female

Nest: cavity; female lines an old woodpecker cavity or a nest box near water; 1 brood per year

Eggs: 10–12; white without markings

Incubation: 32–33 days; female incubates

Fledging: 71 days; female feeds the young

Migration: non-migrator to partial, to southern states; moves around in winter to find open water and food

Food: small fish, aquatic insects, crustaceans (especially crayfish)

Compare: The male Wood Duck (p. 255) has a green head. The male Common Merganser (p. 263) is much larger. The white patch on the head and rust-brown sides distinguish the male Hoodie.

Stan's Notes: A small diving duck, found in shallow ponds, sloughs, lakes and rivers, usually in small groups. Quick, low flight across the water, with fast wingbeats. Male has a deep, rolling call. Female gives a hoarse quack. Nests in wooded areas. Female will lay some eggs in the nests of other mergansers, goldeneyes or Wood Ducks (egg dumping), resulting in 20–25 eggs in some nests. Rarely, she shares a nest, sitting with a Wood Duck.

female
p. 177

male

Ring-necked Duck

Aythya collaris

MIGRATION WINTER

Size: 16–19" (41–48 cm)

Male: Striking black duck with light-gray to white sides. Blue bill with a bold white ring and a thinner ring at the base. Peaked head with a sloped forehead.

Female: brown with darker-brown back and crown, light-brown sides, gray face, white eye-ring, white ring around the bill, and peaked head

Juvenile: similar to female

Nest: ground; female builds; 1 brood per year

Eggs: 8–10; olive to brown without markings

Incubation: 26–27 days; female incubates

Fledging: 49–56 days; female teaches the young to feed

Migration: complete migrator, to southern Ohio and southern states

Food: aquatic plants and insects

Compare: Similar size as the male Lesser Scaup (p. 59), which has a gray back, unlike the black back of the male Ring-necked Duck. Look for the blue bill with a bold white ring to identify the male Ring-necked Duck.

Stan's Notes: Often seen in larger freshwater lakes, usually in small flocks or just pairs. Watch for this diving duck to dive underwater to forage for food. Springs up off the water to take flight. Flattens its crown when diving. Male gives a quick series of grating barks and grunts. Female gives high-pitched peeps. Named "Ring-necked" for its cinnamon collar, which is nearly impossible to see in the field. Also called Ring-billed Duck due to the white ring on its bill.

female
p. 181

male

Common Goldeneye

Bucephala clangula

WINTER

Size: 18–20" (45–51 cm)

Male: Mostly white duck with a black back and a large, puffy, green head. Large white spot on the face. Bright-golden eyes. Dark bill.

Female: Large dark-brown head with a gray body and a white collar. Bright-golden eyes and a yellow-tipped, dark bill.

Juvenile: same as female but has dark eyes

Nest: cavity; female lines an old woodpecker cavity; 1 brood per year

Eggs: 8–10; light green without markings

Incubation: 28–32 days; female incubates

Fledging: 56–59 days; female leads the young to food

Migration: complete, to Ohio, southern states and Mexico

Food: aquatic plants, insects, fish, mollusks

Compare: Similar to the black-and-white male Lesser Scaup (p. 59), which is smaller. Look for the distinctive white spot on the sides of the face and the golden eyes to identify the male Common Goldeneye.

Stan's Notes: Known for the loud whistling sound produced by its wings during flight. During late winter and early spring, the male performs elaborate mating displays that include throwing his head back and calling a raspy note. The female will lay some of her eggs in other goldeneye nests or in the nests of other species (called egg dumping), causing some mothers to incubate as many as 30 eggs in a brood. Named for its bright-golden eyes.

male

female

Pileated Woodpecker
Dryocopus pileatus

YEAR-ROUND

Size: 19" (48 cm)

Male: Crow-size woodpecker with a black back and bright-red forehead, crest and mustache. Long gray bill. White leading edge of wings flashes brightly during flight.

Female: same as male but with a black forehead; lacks a red mustache

Juvenile: similar to adults but duller and browner

Nest: cavity; male and female excavate; 1 brood per year

Eggs: 3–5; white without markings

Incubation: 15–18 days; female incubates during the day, male incubates at night

Fledging: 26–28 days; female and male feed the young

Migration: non-migrator; moves around to find food

Food: insects; will come to suet and peanut feeders

Compare: The Red-headed Woodpecker (p. 55) is about half the size and has an all-red head. Look for the bright-red crest and exceptionally large size to identify the Pileated Woodpecker.

Stan's Notes: Our largest woodpecker. The common name comes from the Latin *pileatus*, which means "wearing a cap." A relatively shy bird that prefers large tracts of woodland. Drums on hollow branches, chimneys and so forth to announce its territory. Excavates oval holes up to several feet long in tree trunks, looking for insects to eat. Large wood chips lie on the ground by excavated trees. Favorite food is carpenter ants. Feeds regurgitated insects to its young. Young emerge from the nest looking just like the adults.

soaring

Osprey
Pandion haliaetus

SUMMER MIGRATION

Size: 21–24" (53–61 cm); up to 5½' wingspan

Male: Large eagle-like bird with a white chest, belly and head. Dark eye line. Nearly black back. Black "wrist" marks on the wings. Dark bill.

Female: same as male but slightly larger and with a necklace of brown streaks

Juvenile: similar to adults, with a light-tan breast

Nest: platform on a raised wooden platform, man-made tower or tall dead tree; female and male build; 1 brood per year

Eggs: 2–4; white with brown markings

Incubation: 32–42 days; female and male incubate

Fledging: 48–58 days; male and female feed the young

Migration: complete, to southern states, Mexico, and Central and South America

Food: fish

Compare: The juvenile Bald Eagle (p. 73) is brown with white speckles. The adult Bald Eagle has an all-white head and tail. Look for the white belly and dark eye line to identify the Osprey.

Stan's Notes: The only species in its family, and the only raptor that plunges into water feetfirst to catch fish. Always near water. Can hover for a few seconds before diving. Carries fish in a head-first position for better aerodynamics. Wings angle back in flight. Often harassed by Bald Eagles for its catch. Gives a high-pitched, whistle-like call, often calling in flight as a warning. Mates have a long-term pair bond. Northern birds may not migrate to the same wintering ground. Was nearly extinct but is now doing well.

winter

breeding

Common Loon
Gavia immer

Size: 28–36" (71–91 cm)

Male: Checkerboard back, black head, white neck-lace. Deep-red eyes. Long, pointed black bill. Winter plumage has a gray body and bill.

Female: same as male

Juvenile: similar to winter plumage but lacks red eyes

Nest: ground, usually at the shoreline; female and male build; 1 brood per year

Eggs: 2; olive brown; occasionally brown markings

Incubation: 26–31 days; female and male incubate

Fledging: 75–80 days; female and male feed the young

Migration: complete, to southern states, the Gulf Coast and Mexico

Food: fish, aquatic insects, crayfish, salamanders

Compare: The Double-crested Cormorant (p. 43) has a black chest and gray bill with a hooked tip and yellow at the base. Look for the checker-board back to identify the Common Loon.

Stan's Notes: Hunts for fish by sight; and prefers clear, clean lakes. A great swimmer, but its legs are set so far back that it has a hard time walking. "Loon" comes from the Scandinavian *lom*, meaning "lame," for the awkward way it walks. To take off, it faces into the wind and runs on the water while flapping. Its wailing call suggests wild laughter, which led to the phrase "crazy as a loon." Also gives soft hoots. In the water, young ride on their parents' backs for about 10 days. Adults perform distraction displays to protect the young. Very sensitive to disturbance during nesting and will abandon the nest. Seen only during spring and fall migration in Ohio.

soaring

juvenile

soaring
juvenile

Bald Eagle
Haliaeetus leucocephalus

YEAR-ROUND MIGRATION

Size: 31–37" (79–94 cm); up to 7½' wingspan

Male: White head and tail contrast sharply with the dark-brown to black body and wings. Large, curved yellow bill and yellow feet.

Female: same as male but larger

Juvenile: dark brown with white speckles and spots on the body and wings; gray bill

Nest: massive platform, usually in a tree; female and male build; 1 brood per year

Eggs: 2–3; off-white without markings

Incubation: 34–36 days; female and male incubate

Fledging: 75–90 days; female and male feed the young

Migration: partial to non-migrator; moves around in winter to find food

Food: fish, carrion, birds (mainly ducks)

Compare: The Turkey Vulture (p. 41) is smaller, has two-toned wings and holds them in a V shape in flight. The Eagle holds its wings straight out.

Stan's Notes: Nearly became extinct due to DDT poisoning and illegal killing. Now making a comeback in North America. Returns to the same nest each year, adding more sticks and enlarging it to huge proportions, at times up to 1,000 pounds (450 kg). In their midair mating ritual, one eagle flips upside down and locks talons with another. Both tumble, then break apart to continue flight. Not uncommon for juveniles to perform this mating ritual even though they have not reached breeding age. Long-term pair bond but will switch mates when not successful at reproducing. Juveniles attain the white head and tail at 4–5 years of age.

female
p. 107

male

Indigo Bunting
Passerina cyanea

SUMMER

Size:	5½" (14 cm)
Male:	Vibrant-blue finch-like bird. Dark markings scattered on wings and tail.
Female:	light-brown with faint markings
Juvenile:	similar to female
Nest:	cup; female builds; 2 broods per year
Eggs:	3–4; pale blue without markings
Incubation:	12–13 days; female incubates
Fledging:	10–11 days; female feeds the young
Migration:	complete, to Florida, Mexico, and Central and South America
Food:	insects, seeds, fruit; will visit seed feeders
Compare:	The male Eastern Bluebird (p. 81) is larger and has a rust-red chest. Look for the bright-blue plumage to identify the male Indigo Bunting.

Stan's Notes: Seen along woodland edges and in parks and yards, feeding on insects. Comes to seed feeders early in spring, before insects are plentiful. Usually only the males are noticed. The male often sings from treetops to attract a mate. The female is quiet. Actually a gray bird, without blue pigment in its feathers: like Blue Jays and other blue birds, sunlight is refracted within the structure of the feathers, making them appear blue. Plumage is iridescent in direct sun, duller in shade. Molts in spring to acquire body feathers with gray tips, which quickly wear off, revealing the bright-blue plumage. Molts in fall and appears like the female during winter. Migrates at night in flocks of 5–10 birds. Males return before the females and juveniles, often to the nest site of the preceding year. Juveniles move to within a mile of their birth site.

Tree Swallow
Tachycineta bicolor

SUMMER

Size: 5–6" (13–15 cm)

Male: Blue green in spring, greener in fall. Changes color in direct sunlight. White from chin to belly. Long, pointed wing tips. Notched tail.

Female: similar to male but duller

Juvenile: grayish brown with a white belly and a grayish breast band

Nest: cavity; female and male line a vacant woodpecker cavity or nest box; 2 broods per year

Eggs: 4–6; white without markings

Incubation: 13–16 days; female incubates

Fledging: 20–24 days; female and male feed the young

Migration: complete, to Mexico and Central America

Food: insects

Compare: The Purple Martin (p. 83) is much larger and darker. The Barn Swallow (p. 79) has a rusty belly and a long, deeply forked tail. Look for the white chin, chest and belly and the notched tail to help identify the Tree Swallow.

Stan's Notes: Found at ponds, lakes, rivers and farm fields. Often seen flying back and forth across fields, feeding on insects. Can be attracted to your yard with a nest box. Competes with the Eastern Bluebird for tree cavities and nest boxes. Builds a grass nest within and will travel long distances, looking for dropped feathers for the lining. Watch for it playing and chasing after feathers. Flies with rapid wingbeats, then glides. Gives a series of gurgles and chirps. Chatters when upset or threatened. Eats many nuisance bugs. Families gather in large flocks for migration.

Barn Swallow
Hirundo rustica

SUMMER

Size: 7" (18 cm)

Male: Sleek swallow. Blue-black back, cinnamon belly and reddish-brown chin. White spots on a long, deeply forked tail.

Female: same as male but with a whitish belly

Juvenile: similar to adults, with a tan belly and chin and a shorter tail

Nest: cup; female and male build; 2 broods per year

Eggs: 4–5; white with brown markings

Incubation: 13–17 days; female incubates

Fledging: 18–23 days; female and male feed the young

Migration: complete, to South America

Food: insects (prefers beetles, wasps, flies)

Compare: The Tree Swallow (p. 77) is white from chin to belly. The Purple Martin (p. 83) is larger and has a dark-purple belly. The Chimney Swift (p. 93) has a narrow, pointed tail. Look for the deeply forked tail to identify the Barn Swallow.

Stan's Notes: Seen in wetlands, farms, suburban yards and parks. Ohio has six swallow species, but this is the only one with a deeply forked tail. Unlike other swallows, it rarely glides in flight. Usually flies low over land or water. Drinks as it flies, skimming water, or will sip water droplets on wet leaves. Bathes while flying through rain or sprinklers. Gives a twittering warble, followed by a mechanical sound. Builds a mud nest with up to 1,000 beak-loads of mud. Nests on barns and houses, under bridges and in other sheltered places. Often nests in colonies of 4–6 birds; sometimes nests alone.

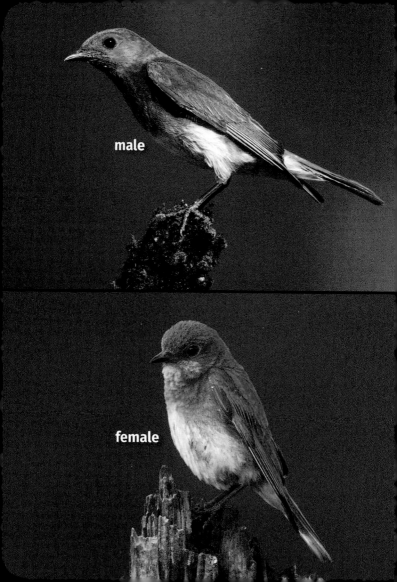

male

female

Eastern Bluebird
Sialia sialis

YEAR-ROUND SUMMER

Size: 7" (18 cm)

Male: Sky-blue head, back and tail. Rust-red breast and white belly.

Female: grayer than male, with a faint rusty breast and faint blue wings and tail

Juvenile: similar to female but with spots on the breast and blue wing markings

Nest: cavity, vacant woodpecker cavity or nest box; female adds a soft lining; 2 broods per year

Eggs: 4–5; pale blue without markings

Incubation: 12–14 days; female incubates

Fledging: 15–18 days; male and female feed the young

Migration: non-migrator to complete, to southern states

Food: insects, fruit; comes to shallow dishes with live or dead mealworms, and to suet feeders

Compare: The male Indigo Bunting (p. 75) is nearly all blue. The Blue Jay (p. 85) is much larger and has a crest. Look for the rusty breast to help identify the Eastern Bluebird.

Stan's Notes: Nearly eliminated from Ohio due to a lack of nest cavities. Thanks to people who installed thousands of nest boxes, bluebirds now thrive. Prefers open habitats, such as farm fields, pastures and roadsides, but also likes forest edges, parks and yards. Easily tamed. Often perches on trees or fence posts and drops to the ground to grab bugs, especially grasshoppers. Makes short flights from tree to tree. Song is a distinctive "churlee chur chur-lee." The rust-red breast is like that of the American Robin, its cousin. The young of the first brood help raise the second brood.

Purple Martin

Progne subis

Size: 8½" (21.5 cm)

Male: iridescent with a purple to black head, back and belly; black wings; and a notched black tail

Female: grayish-purple head and back, darker wings and tail, whitish belly

Juvenile: same as female

Nest: cavity; female and male line the cavity of the house; 1 brood per year

Eggs: 4–5; white without markings

Incubation: 15–18 days; female incubates

Fledging: 26–30 days; male and female feed the young

Migration: complete, to South America

Food: insects

Compare: Usually seen only in groups. The male Purple Martin is the only swallow with a very dark purplish belly.

Stan's Notes: The largest swallow species in North America. Once nested in tree cavities; now nests almost exclusively in man-made, apartment-style houses. The most successful colonies often nest in multiunit nest boxes within 100 feet (30 m) of a human dwelling near a lake. Main diet consists of dragonflies, not mosquitoes, as once thought. Gives a continuous stream of chirps, creaks and rattles, along with a shout-like "churrr" and chortle. Often drinks in flight, skimming water, and bathes in flight, flying through rain. Returns to the same nest site each year; the males arrive before the females and yearlings. The young leave to form new colonies. Large colonies gather in fall before migrating to South America.

Blue Jay
Cyanocitta cristata

YEAR-ROUND

Size: 12" (30 cm)

Male: Bright light-blue and white bird with a black necklace and gray belly. Large crest moves up and down at will. White face, wing bars and tip of tail. Black tail bands.

Female: same as male

Juvenile: same as adult but duller

Nest: cup; female and male construct; 1–2 broods per year

Eggs: 4–5; green to blue with brown markings

Incubation: 16–18 days; female incubates

Fledging: 17–21 days; female and male feed the young

Migration: non-migrator to partial; will move around in winter to find an abundant food source

Food: insects, fruit, carrion, seeds, nuts; visits seed feeders, ground feeders with corn or peanuts

Compare: The Belted Kingfisher (p. 87) has a larger, more ragged crest. The Eastern Bluebird (p. 81) is much smaller and has a rust-red breast. Look for the large crest to help identify the Blue Jay.

Stan's Notes: Highly intelligent, solving problems, gathering food and communicating more than other birds. Loud and noisy; mimics other birds. Known as the alarm of the forest, screaming at intruders. Imitates hawk calls around feeders to scare off other birds. One of the few birds to cache food; can remember where it hid thousands of nuts. Carries food in a pouch under its tongue (sublingually). Eats eggs and young birds from other nests. Feathers lack blue pigment; refracted sunlight causes the blue appearance.

Belted Kingfisher
Megaceryle alcyon

YEAR-ROUND

Size: 12–14" (30–36 cm)

Male: Blue with white belly, blue-gray chest band, and black wing tips. Ragged crest moves up and down at will. Large head. Long, thick, black bill. White spot by eyes. Red-brown eyes.

Female: same as male but with rusty flanks and a rusty chest band below the blue-gray band

Juvenile: similar to female

Nest: cavity; female and male excavate in a bank of a river, lake or cliff; 1 brood per year

Eggs: 6–7; white without markings

Incubation: 23–24 days; female and male incubate

Fledging: 23–24 days; female and male feed the young

Migration: non-migrator in Ohio; moves around in winter to find open water and food

Food: small fish

Compare: The Blue Jay (p. 85) is lighter blue and has a plain gray chest and belly. The Belted Kingfisher is rarely found away from water.

Stan's Notes: Usually found at the bank of a river, lake or large stream. Perches on a branch near water, dives in headfirst to catch a small fish, then returns to the branch to feed. Parents drop dead fish into the water to teach their young to dive. Can't pass bones through its digestive tract; regurgitates bone pellets after meals. Gives a loud call that sounds like a machine gun. Mates know each other by their calls. Digs a tunnel up to 4 feet (1 m) long to a nest chamber. Small white patches on dark wing tips flash during flight.

Chestnut-sided Warbler

Setophaga pensylvanica

SUMMER MIGRATION

Size: 5" (13 cm)

Male: Colorful combination of a bright-yellow cap, black mask and white face, with a white chest and belly. Chestnut flanks. Gray wings with 2 yellow wing bars. White undertail.

Female: similar to male, with duller brown flanks

Juvenile: similar to female, with a lime-green head and back, white eye-ring and bright-yellow wing bars; lacks chestnut sides

Nest: cup; female builds; 1 brood per year

Eggs: 3–5; white with brown markings

Incubation: 12–13 days; female incubates

Fledging: 10–12 days; female and male feed the young

Migration: complete, to Central America

Food: insects, berries

Compare: The Yellow-rumped Warbler (p. 215) has yellow patches on its sides and rump. The Yellow Warbler (p. 301) is nearly all yellow. Look for the yellow cap and chestnut flanks to help identify the Chestnut-sided Warbler.

Stan's Notes: A very attractive warbler, named for the chestnut patches on its sides. Prefers an open, young aspen forest. During migration, it is often attracted to backyard water gardens that have a small trickling stream. Look for it in spring, hopping high up in trees while it hunts for insects. Usually you will get only a glimpse of this fast-moving bird. Holds tail in an uplifted position, showing the white undertail. It is not uncommon for it to approach people near its nest in defense of the site.

Brown Creeper
Certhia americana

YEAR-ROUND
WINTER

Size: 5" (13 cm)

Male: Small, thin, nearly camouflaged brown bird. White from chin to belly. White eyebrows. Dark eyes and a thin, curved bill. Tail is long and stiff.

Female: same as male

Juvenile: same as adults

Nest: cup; female constructs; 1 brood per year

Eggs: 5–6; white with tiny brown markings

Incubation: 14–17 days; female incubates; male feeds the female during incubation

Fledging: 13–16 days; female and male feed the young

Migration: non-migrator to partial

Food: insects, nuts, seeds

Compare: The Red-breasted Nuthatch (p. 207) and White-breasted Nuthatch (p. 213) climb down tree trunks, not up. To spot a Brown Creeper, look for a small brown bird with a white belly creeping up trees.

Stan's Notes: A forest bird, commonly found in wooded habitats. Will fly from the top of one tree trunk to the bottom of another, then work its way to the top, looking for caterpillars, spider eggs and more. Its long tail has tiny spines underneath, which help it cling to trees. Uses its camouflage coloring to hide in plain sight: it spreads out flat on a branch or trunk and won't move. Often builds its nest behind the loose bark of a dead or dying tree. Young follow their parents around, creeping up trees soon after fledging.

Chimney Swift
Chaetura pelagica

SUMMER

Size: 5" (13 cm)

Male: Nondescript, cigar-shaped bird, usually seen in flight. Long, thin, brown body. Pointed tail and head. Long, backswept wings, longer than the body.

Female: same as male

Juvenile: same as adults

Nest: half cup; female and male construct; 1 brood per year

Eggs: 4–5; white without markings

Incubation: 19–21 days; female and male incubate

Fledging: 28–30 days; female and male feed the young

Migration: complete, to South America

Food: insects caught in midair

Compare: The Purple Martin (p. 83) is much larger and darker. The Barn Swallow (p. 79) has a deeply forked tail. Tree Swallows (p. 77) have a white belly and blue-green back. Look for the cigar shape to identify the Chimney Swift in flight.

Stan's Notes: One of the fastest fliers in the bird world. Spends all day flying, rarely perching. Flies in groups, feeding on insects flying 100 feet (30 m) or higher up in the air. Often called a Flying Cigar due to its body shape, which is pointed at both ends. Drinks and bathes during flight, skimming water. Gives a unique in-flight twittering call, often heard before the bird is seen. Hundreds roost in large chimneys, giving it the common name. Builds its nest with tiny twigs, cementing it with saliva and attaching it to the inside of a chimney or a hollow tree. Usually only one nest per chimney.

Chipping Sparrow

Spizella passerina

SUMMER

Size:	5" (13 cm)
Male:	Small gray-brown sparrow with clear-gray chest, white eyebrows, thin black eye line and rusty crown. Thin gray-black bill. 2 faint wing bars.
Female:	same as male
Juvenile:	similar to adults, with streaking on the chest; lacks a rusty crown
Nest:	cup; female builds; 2 broods per year
Eggs:	3–5; blue-green with brown markings
Incubation:	11–14 days; female incubates
Fledging:	10–12 days; female and male feed the young
Migration:	complete, to southern states, Mexico and Central America
Food:	insects, seeds; will come to ground feeders
Compare:	The American Tree Sparrow (p. 113) has gray eyebrows and a rusty eye line. The Song Sparrow (p. 111), Fox Sparrow (p. 123) and female House Finch (p. 101) have heavily streaked chests. The rusty crown and black eye line help identify the Chipping Sparrow.

Stan's Notes: A common garden or yard bird, often seen feeding on dropped seeds beneath feeders. Gathers in large family groups to feed in preparation for migration. Migrates at night in flocks of 20–30 birds. The common name comes from the male's fast "chip" call. Often just called a Chippy. Builds nest low in dense shrubs and almost always lines it with animal hair. Comfortable with people, allowing you to approach closely before it flies away.

male

Hoary Redpoll

female

Common Redpoll
Acanthis flammea

WINTER

Size: 5" (13 cm)

Male: Sparrow-like bird with a bright-red crown and raspberry red on the chest. Black spot on the chin. Heavily streaked back.

Female: similar to male but lacks red on the chest

Juvenile: browner than adults, with dark streaking on the chest; lacks a red crown

Nest: cup; female builds; 1 brood (occasionally 2) per year

Eggs: 4–5; pale green with purple markings

Incubation: 10–11 days; female incubates

Fledging: 11–12 days; female and male feed the young

Migration: irruptive; moves into Ohio from the far reaches of Canada in some winters

Food: seeds, insects; will come to seed feeders

Compare: The Pine Siskin (p. 99) has yellow wing bars and a streaked chest. Look for the bright-red crown and black spot under the bill to help identify the Common Redpoll. The male House Finch (p. 271) has large gray bill.

Stan's Notes: Moves from location to location, wheeling around in the sky before landing at feeders. Visits feeders in small to large flocks. Flocks of up 100 birds are not uncommon but are not seen at all in some winters. Bathes in open water or snow in winter. Like the Black-capped Chickadee, it can be tamed and fed by hand. Gives a zipping call in long strings that last 30 seconds or more. Also gives a nasal, rising whistle. The Hoary Redpoll (inset) is paler with less streaking on the flanks and a pink wash on the chest.

Pine Siskin
Spinus pinus

Size: 5" (13 cm)

Male: Small brown finch with heavy streaking on the back, breast and belly. Yellow wing bars. Yellow at the base of the tail. Thin bill.

Female: similar to male, with less yellow

Juvenile: similar to adult, with a light-yellow tinge over the breast and chin

Nest: cup; female builds; 2 broods

Eggs: 3–4; greenish blue with brown markings

Incubation: 12–13 days; female incubates

Fledging: 14–15 days; female and male feed the young

Migration: irruptive; moves into Ohio in winter and around the U.S. in search of food

Food: seeds, insects; will come to seed feeders

Compare: The female Purple Finch (p. 117) has white eyebrows. The female House Finch (p. 101) lacks yellow. The female American Goldfinch (p. 293) has white wing bars. Look for the yellow wing bars to identify the Pine Siskin.

Stan's Notes: Usually considered a winter finch. Conspicuous in some winters, rare in others. Seen in flocks of up to 20 birds, often with other finch species. Gathers in flocks and moves around, visiting feeders. Will come to thistle feeders. Gives a series of high-pitched, wheezy calls. Also gives a wheezing twitter. Breeds in small groups. Builds nest toward the end of coniferous branches, where needles are dense, helping to conceal. Nests are often only a few feet apart. Male feeds the female during incubation. Juveniles lose the yellow tint by late summer of their first year.

male
p. 271

female

House Finch

Haemorhous mexicanus

YEAR-ROUND

Size:	5" (13 cm)
Female:	plain brown with heavy streaking on a white chest
Male:	red to orange face, throat, chest and rump; brown cap; brown marking behind the eyes; streaked belly and wings
Juvenile:	similar to female
Nest:	cup, occasionally in a cavity; female builds; 2 broods per year
Eggs:	4–5; pale blue, lightly marked
Incubation:	12–14 days; female incubates
Fledging:	15–19 days; female and male feed the young
Migration:	non-migrator to partial; will move around to find food
Food:	seeds, fruit, leaf buds; visits seed feeders and feeders that offer grape jelly
Compare:	The female Purple Finch (p. 117) has bold white eyebrows. The Pine Siskin (p. 99) has yellow wing bars and a smaller bill. The female American Goldfinch (p. 293) has a clear chest. Look for the heavily streaked chest to help identify the female House Finch.

Stan's Notes: Can be a common bird at your feeders. A very social bird, visiting feeders in small flocks. Likes to nest in hanging flower baskets. Male sings a loud, cheerful warbling song. It was originally introduced to Long Island, New York, from the western U.S. in the 1940s. Now found throughout the country. Suffers from a disease that causes the eyes to crust, resulting in blindness and death.

House Wren
Troglodytes aedon

SUMMER

Size: 5" (13 cm)

Male: All-brown bird with lighter-brown markings on the wings and tail. Slightly curved brown bill. Often holds tail upward.

Female: same as male

Juvenile: same as adults

Nest: cavity; female and male line just about any nest cavity; 2 broods per year

Eggs: 4–6; tan with brown markings

Incubation: 10–13 days; female and male incubate

Fledging: 12–15 days; female and male feed the young

Migration: complete, to southern states and Mexico

Food: insects, spiders, snails

Compare: The slightly curved bill and upward position of the tail differentiate the House Wren from sparrows. All other species of wrens have eyebrows.

Stan's Notes: A prolific songster. During the mating season, sings from dawn to dusk. Seen in brushy yards, parks and woodlands and along forest edges. Easily attracted to a nest box. In spring, the male chooses several prospective nesting cavities and places a few small twigs in each. The female inspects all of them and finishes constructing the nest in the cavity of her choice. She fills the cavity with short twigs and then lines a small depression at the back with pine needles and grass. She often has trouble fitting longer twigs through the entrance hole and tries many different directions and approaches until she is successful.

103

Carolina Wren
Thryothorus ludovicianus

Size: 5½" (14 cm)

Male: Rusty-brown head and back with an orange-yellow chest and belly. White throat and a prominent white eye stripe. Short, stubby tail, often cocked up.

Female: same as male

Juvenile: same as adults

Nest: cavity; female and male build; 2 broods per year, sometimes 3

Eggs: 4–6; white, sometimes pink or creamy, with brown markings

Incubation: 12–14 days; female incubates

Fledging: 12–14 days; female and male feed young

Migration: non-migrator to partial; moves around to find food

Food: insects, fruit, few seeds; visits suet feeders

Compare: Similar to the House Wren (p. 103), but Carolina Wren is lighter brown and has a prominent white eye stripe.

Stan's Notes: Mates are long-term, staying together throughout the year in permanent territories. Sings year-round. The male is known to sing up to 40 song types, singing one song repeatedly before switching to another. The female also sings, resulting in duets. The male often takes over feeding the first brood while the female renests. Nests in birdhouses and in unusual places like mailboxes, bumpers or broken taillights of vehicles, or nearly any other cavity. Found in brushy yards or woodlands. Can be attracted to feeders with mealworms.

female

male
p. 75

Indigo Bunting
Passerina cyanea

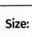

SUMMER

Size: 5½" (14 cm)

Female: Light-brown, finch-like bird. Faint streaking on a light-tan chest. Wings have a very faint blue cast and indistinct wing bars.

Male: vibrant blue with scattered dark markings on wings and tail

Juvenile: similar to female

Nest: cup; female builds; 2 broods per year

Eggs: 3–4; pale blue without markings

Incubation: 12–13 days; female incubates

Fledging: 10–11 days; female feeds the young

Migration: complete, to southern Florida, Mexico, and Central and South America

Food: insects, seeds, fruit; will visit seed feeders

Compare: The female Purple Finch (p. 117) has white eyebrows and heavy streaking on the chest. The female House Finch (p. 101) has a heavily streaked chest. The female American Goldfinch (p. 293) has white wing bars. Look for the faint blue cast on the wings to help identify the female Indigo Bunting.

Stan's Notes: Seen along woodland edges and in parks and yards, feeding on insects. Comes to seed feeders early in spring, before insects are plentiful. Secretive, plain and quiet; usually only the males are noticed. The male often sings from treetops to attract a mate. Migrates at night in flocks of 5–10 birds. Males return before the females and juveniles, often to the nest site of the preceding year. Juveniles move to within a mile of their birth site.

male
p. 217

female

Dark-eyed Junco

Junco hyemalis

YEAR-ROUND
WINTER

Size: 5½" (14 cm)

Female: Plump, dark-eyed bird with a tan to brown chest, head and back. White belly. Ivory to pink bill. White outer tail feathers appear like a white V in flight.

Male: round with gray plumage

Juvenile: similar to female, with streaking on the breast and head

Nest: cup; female and male build; 2 broods per year

Eggs: 3–5; white with reddish-brown markings

Incubation: 12–13 days; female incubates

Fledging: 10–13 days; male and female feed the young

Migration: complete, throughout the U.S.

Food: seeds, insects; visits ground and seed feeders

Compare: Rarely confused with any other bird. Look for the ivory to pink bill and small flocks feeding under feeders to help identify the female Dark-eyed Junco.

Stan's Notes: One of the most common winter birds in the state. Migrates from Canada to Ohio and areas farther south. Adheres to a rigid social hierarchy, with dominant birds chasing the less dominant ones. Look for the white outer tail feathers flashing in flight. Often seen in small flocks on the ground, where it uses its feet to simultaneously "double-scratch" to expose seeds and insects. Eats many weed seeds. Nests in a wide variety of wooded habitats. Several subspecies of Dark-eyed Junco were previously considered to be separate species.

Song Sparrow
Melospiza melodia

Size: 5–6" (13–15 cm)

Male: Common brown sparrow with heavy dark streaks on the chest coalescing into a central dark spot.

Female: same as male

Juvenile: similar to adults, with a finely streaked chest; lacks a central dark spot

Nest: cup; female builds; 2 broods per year

Eggs: 3–4; blue to green, with red-brown markings

Incubation: 12–14 days; female incubates

Fledging: 9–12 days; female and male feed the young

Migration: non-migrator; moves around to find food

Food: insects, seeds; only rarely comes to ground feeders with seeds

Compare: Similar to other brown sparrows. Look for the heavily streaked chest with a central dark spot to help identify the Song Sparrow.

Stan's Notes: There are many subspecies of this bird, but the dark spot in the center of the chest appears in every variety. A constant songster, repeating its loud, clear song every few minutes. The song varies from region to region but has the same basic structure. Sings from thick shrubs to defend a small territory, beginning with three notes and finishing up with a trill. A ground feeder, it will "double-scratch" with both feet at the same time to expose seeds. When the female builds a new nest for a second brood, the male often takes over feeding the first brood. Unlike many other sparrow species, Song Sparrows rarely flock together. A common host of the Brown-headed Cowbird.

American Tree Sparrow
Spizelloides arborea

WINTER

Size: 6" (15 cm)

Male: Brown with a tan chest and rusty crown and eye line. Gray eyebrows. Dark spot in the center of the chest. Dark upper bill; yellow lower bill. 2 white wing bars.

Female: same as male

Juvenile: streaked chest often obscures the central dark spot; lacks a rusty crown

Nest: cup; female builds; 1 brood per year

Eggs: 3–5; greenish white with brown markings

Incubation: 12–13 days; female incubates

Fledging: 8–10 days; female and male feed the young

Migration: complete, to Ohio and most of the U.S., from Canada

Food: insects, seeds; visits seed feeders

Compare: The Chipping Sparrow (p. 95) has white eyebrows and a black eye line. The Song Sparrow (p. 111) has a heavily streaked chest. To identify the American Tree Sparrow, check for the dark spot on the chest and the two-toned bill.

Stan's Notes: A regular feeder visitor throughout Ohio during winter. Seen during migration in flocks of 2–200 birds. Found in open fields, woodlands and suburban backyards. Sometimes called a Winter Chippy because it looks like the Chipping Sparrow. Gives a series of high-pitched, sweet-sounding whistles. Nests in Canada and Alaska. The species name *arborea* means "tree," but it doesn't nest in trees; it nests on the ground in a clump of grass. The "Tree" in the name refers to its habitat. "American" refers to its natural range.

male

female

House Sparrow
Passer domesticus

YEAR-ROUND

Size:	6" (15 cm)
Male:	Brown back with a gray belly and cap. Large black patch extending from the throat to the chest (bib). 1 white wing bar.
Female:	slightly smaller than the male, light brown with light eyebrows; lacks a bib and white wing bar
Juvenile:	similar to female
Nest:	cavity; female and male build a domed cup nest within; 2–3 broods per year
Eggs:	4–6; white with brown markings
Incubation:	10–12 days; female incubates
Fledging:	14–17 days; female and male feed the young
Migration:	non-migrator; moves around to find food
Food:	seeds, insects, fruit; comes to seed feeders
Compare:	The American Tree Sparrow (p. 113) and the Chipping Sparrow (p. 95) have a rusty crown. Look for the black bib to identify the male House Sparrow and the clear breast to help identify the female.

Stan's Notes: One of the first birdsongs heard in cities in spring. A familiar city bird, nearly always in small flocks. Also found on farms. Introduced in 1850 from Europe to Central Park in New York. Now seen throughout North America. Related to old-world sparrows; not a relative of any sparrows in the U.S. An aggressive bird that will kill young birds in order to take over the nest cavity. Uses dried grass and small scraps of plastic, paper and other materials to build an oversize, domed nest in the cavity.

male
p. 273

female

Purple Finch
Haemorhous purpureus

YEAR-ROUND WINTER

Size:	6" (15 cm)
Female:	plain brown with heavy streaking on the chest, bold white eyebrows and a large bill
Male:	raspberry-red head, cap, breast, back and rump; brownish wings and tail
Juvenile:	same as female
Nest:	cup; female and male build; 1 brood per year
Eggs:	4–5; greenish blue with brown markings
Incubation:	12–13 days; female incubates
Fledging:	13–14 days; female and male feed the young
Migration:	irruptive; moves around in winter to find food
Food:	seeds, insects, fruit; comes to seed feeders
Compare:	The female House Finch (p. 101) lacks eyebrows. The Pine Siskin (p. 99) has yellow wing bars. The female American Goldfinch (p. 293) has a clear chest. Look for the bold white eyebrows to identify the female Purple Finch.

Stan's Notes: A year-round resident of northeastern Ohio. More commonly seen during winter in the rest of the state. Long-term residency in Ohio, unlike the recent invasion of the House Finch. Travels in flocks of up to 50 birds. Visits seed feeders along with House Finches, which makes it hard to tell them apart. Feeds mainly on seeds; ash tree seeds are an important source of food. Found in coniferous forests, mixed woods, woodland edges and suburban backyards. Flies in the typical undulating, up-and-down pattern of finches. Sings a rich, loud song. Gives a distinctive "tic" note only in flight. The male is not purple. The Latin species name *purpureus* means "purple" (and other reddish colors).

WINTER

White-throated Sparrow
Zonotrichia albicollis

Size: 6–7" (15–18 cm)

Male: Brown with a gray or tan chest and belly and a white or tan throat patch and eyebrows. Bold striping on the head. Small yellow spot in the space between the eye and bill, called the lore.

Female: same as male

Juvenile: similar to adults, with a heavily streaked chest and a gray throat and eyebrows

Nest: cup; female builds; 1 brood per year

Eggs: 4–6; green to blue, or cream white with red-brown markings

Incubation: 11–14 days; female incubates

Fledging: 10–12 days; female and male feed the young

Migration: complete, to Ohio, southern states and Mexico

Food: insects, seeds, fruit; visits ground feeders

Compare: The White-crowned Sparrow (p. 121) lacks the throat patch and yellow lores of the White-throated Sparrow.

Stan's Notes: Two color variations (polymorphic): white striped and tan striped. Studies indicate that the white-striped adults tend to mate with the tan-striped birds; it's not clear why. Known for its wonderful song; it sings all year and can even be heard at night. White- and tan-striped males and white-striped females sing, but tan-striped females do not. Builds nest on the ground under small trees in bogs and coniferous forests. Often associated with other sparrows in winter. Feeds on the ground under feeders. Immature and first-year females tend to winter farther south than adults.

juvenile

WINTER

White-crowned Sparrow
Zonotrichia leucophrys

Size: 6½–7½" (16.5–19 cm)

Male: Brown with a gray chest and black-and-white striped crown. Small, thin, pink or yellow bill.

Female: same as male

Juvenile: similar to adults, with black and brown stripes on the head

Nest: cup; female builds; 2 broods per year

Eggs: 3–5; greenish to bluish to whitish with red-brown markings

Incubation: 11–14 days; female incubates

Fledging: 8–12 days; male and female feed the young

Migration: complete, to Ohio, southern states, and Mexico

Food: insects, seeds, berries; visits ground feeders

Compare: The White-throated Sparrow (p. 119) has a throat patch and a small yellow spot by each eye. The Song Sparrow (p. 111) has a streaked chest. Look for the striped crown to help identify the White-crowned Sparrow.

Stan's Notes: Often in groups of up to 20 birds during winter, when it can be seen visiting ground feeders and feeding beneath seed feeders. This ground feeder will "double-scratch" backward with both feet simultaneously to find seeds. Prefers scrubby areas, woodland edges, and open or grassy habitats. The males are prolific songsters, singing in late winter while migrating north. Males arrive at the breeding grounds before the females and sing from perches to establish territory. Males take most of the responsibility for raising the young while females start their second broods. Only 9–12 days separate the broods. Nests in Canada and Alaska.

Fox Sparrow
Passerella iliaca

MIGRATION
WINTER

Size:	7" (18 cm)
Male:	Plump, rust-red sparrow. Heavily streaked, rusty breast and solid-rust tail. Head and back are mottled with gray.
Female:	same as male
Juvenile:	same as adults
Nest:	cup; female builds; 2 broods per year
Eggs:	2–4; pale green with reddish markings
Incubation:	12–14 days; female incubates
Fledging:	10–11 days; female and male feed the young
Migration:	complete, to southern states and the south-western corner of Ohio
Food:	seeds, insects; comes to ground feeders
Compare:	The Brown Thrasher (p. 153) is much larger, is slimmer and has a long, curved bill. The rust-red plumage of the Fox Sparrow differentiates it from all other sparrows.

Stan's Notes: One of the largest sparrows. Often seen alone or in small groups. Found in shrubby areas, open fields and backyards. Comes to ground feeders; searches for seeds and insects underneath seed feeders during migration. Like a chicken, it will "double-scratch" with both feet at the same time to look for food. Gives a series of rich notes lasting 2–3 seconds, usually singing from a perch hidden in a shrub. The common name "Sparrow" comes from the Anglo-Saxon word *spearwa*, meaning "flutterer," as applies to any small bird. "Fox" refers to its rusty color. Appears in several color variations, depending on location. Nests on the ground in brush and along forest edges in Canada and Alaska.

female

male
p. 23

Eastern Towhee
Pipilo erythrophthalmus

YEAR-ROUND SUMMER

Size: 7–8" (18–20 cm)

Female: Mostly light-brown bird. Rusty red-brown sides and a white belly. Long brown tail with a white tip. Short, stout, pointed bill and rich-red eyes. White wing patches flash in flight.

Male: similar to female but black instead of brown

Juvenile: Light brown with a heavily streaked head, chest and belly. Long dark tail with a white tip.

Nest: cup; female builds; 2 broods per year

Eggs: 3–4; cream-white with brown markings

Incubation: 12–13 days; female incubates

Fledging: 10–12 days; male and female feed young

Migration: non-migrator to partial, to southern Ohio and southern states

Food: insects, seeds, fruit; visits ground feeders

Compare: Smaller than the American Robin (p. 231), which has a red breast and lacks the white belly. The female Rose-breasted Grosbeak (p. 133) has a heavily streaked breast and obvious white eyebrows.

Stan's Notes: Named for its distinctive "tow-hee" call, given by both sexes, but known mostly for its other characteristic call, which sounds like "drink-your-tea!" Will hop backward with both feet (double-scratching), raking up leaf litter to locate insects and seeds. The female does the brooding. The male feeds the young most of the time.

male
p. 25

female

Brown-headed Cowbird
Molothrus ater

Size:	7½" (19 cm)
Female:	Dull brown with no obvious markings. Pointed, sharp, gray bill. Dark eyes.
Male:	glossy black with a chocolate-brown head
Juvenile:	similar to female but with dull-gray plumage and a streaked chest
Nest:	no nest; lays eggs in the nests of other birds
Eggs:	5–7; white with brown markings
Incubation:	10–13 days; host birds incubate the eggs
Fledging:	10–11 days; host birds feed the young
Migration:	non-migrator in Ohio; moves around to find food
Food:	insects, seeds; will come to seed feeders
Compare:	The female Red-winged Blackbird (p. 139) has white eyebrows and heavy streaking. The female Indigo Bunting (p. 107) has faint blue on its wings. The pointed gray bill helps to identify the female Brown-headed Cowbird.

Stan's Notes: Cowbirds are members of the blackbird family. Known as brood parasites, Brown-headed Cowbirds are the only parasitic birds in Ohio. Brood parasites lay their eggs in the nests of other birds, leaving the host birds to raise their young. Cowbirds are known to have laid their eggs in the nests of over 200 species of birds. While some birds reject cowbird eggs, most incubate them and raise the young, even to the exclusion of their own. Look for warblers and other birds feeding young birds twice their own size. Named "Cowbird" for its habit of following bison and cattle herds to feed on insects flushed up by the animals.

1 year
old

Bohemian
Waxwing

Cedar Waxwing

Bombycilla cedrorum

YEAR-ROUND

Size: 7½" (19 cm)

Male: Sleek-looking, gray to brown bird. Pointed crest, bandit-like mask and light-yellow belly. Bold-yellow tip of tail. Red wing tips look like they were dipped in red wax.

Female: same as male

Juvenile: grayish with a heavily streaked breast; lacks the sleek look, black mask and red wing tips

Nest: cup; female and male construct; 1 brood per year, occasionally 2

Eggs: 4–6; pale blue with brown markings

Incubation: 10–12 days; female incubates

Fledging: 14–18 days; female and male feed the young

Migration: partial migrator; moves around to find food

Food: cedar cones, fruit, seeds, insects

Compare: The female Northern Cardinal (p. 137) has a large red bill. The Bohemian Waxwing (inset), is larger and less common and has white on its wings and rust under its tail. Look for the red wing tips to identify the Cedar Waxwing.

Stan's Notes: The name is derived from its red, wax-like wing tips and preference for the small, berry-like cones of the cedar. Seen in flocks, moving around from area to area looking for berries. Feeds on insects during summer, before berries are abundant. Wanders during winter, searching for food supplies. Spends most of its time at the top of tall trees. Listen for the high-pitched "sreee" whistling sound it constantly makes while perched or in flight. Obtains the mask after the first year and red wing tips after the second year.

female

male

Horned Lark
Eremophila alpestris

YEAR-ROUND

Size: 7–8" (18–20 cm)

Male: Tan to brown with black markings on the face. Black necklace and bill. Pale-yellow chin. Two tiny feather "horns" on the top of the head, sometimes hard to see. Dark tail with white outer tail feathers, seen in flight.

Female: duller than male; less noticeable "horns"

Juvenile: lacks a yellow chin and black markings; does not develop "horns" until the second year

Nest: ground; female builds; 2–3 broods per year

Eggs: 3–4; gray with brown markings

Incubation: 11–12 days; female incubates

Fledging: 9–12 days; female and male feed the young

Migration: non-migrator to partial in Ohio; moves around to find food

Food: seeds, insects

Compare: The Eastern Meadowlark (p. 313) has a yellow breast and belly. Look for the black markings by the eyes and the black necklace.

Stan's Notes: The only true lark native to North America. A bird of open ground. Common in rural areas; often seen in large flocks. The population increased in North America over the past century as more land was cleared for farming. Male performs a fluttering courtship flight high in the air while singing a high-pitched song. Female performs a fluttering distraction display when the nest is disturbed. Starts breeding early in the year. Able to renest about a week after the brood fledges. Moves around in winter to find food. "Lark" comes from the Middle English *laverock*, or "a lark."

female

male
p. 49

Rose-breasted Grosbeak

Pheucticus ludovicianus

SUMMER MIGRATION

Size: 7–8" (18–20 cm)

Female: Plump and heavily streaked. Large, obvious white eyebrows. Large ivory bill. Orange to yellow wing linings.

Male: black and white with a triangular rose patch in the center of the chest, rose wing linings

Juvenile: similar to female

Nest: cup; female and male construct; 1–2 broods per year

Eggs: 3–5; blue green with brown markings

Incubation: 13–14 days; female and male incubate

Fledging: 9–12 days; female and male feed the young

Migration: complete, to Mexico, Central America and South America

Food: insects, seeds, fruit; comes to seed feeders

Compare: Looks like a large finch with bold white eyebrows and heavy streaking. The female Purple Finch (p. 117) has smaller eyebrows. The female House Finch (p. 101) lacks eyebrows.

Stan's Notes: Seen in small groups. Prefers a mature deciduous forest for nesting. Both sexes sing, but the male sings much louder and clearer. Sings a rich, robin-like song with a chip note in the tune. "Grosbeak" refers to the thick, strong bill, which is used to crush seeds. Males arrive at the breeding grounds a few days before females. Several males will visit seed feeders together in spring. When females arrive, males become territorial and reduce their feeder visits. After fledging, the young visit feeders with the adults. Makes short flights from tree to tree with rapid wingbeats.

winter

breeding

Spotted Sandpiper

Actitis macularius

SUMMER

Size: 8" (20 cm)

Male: Olive-brown back with black spots on a white chest and belly. White line over eyes. Long, dull-yellow legs. Long bill. Winter plumage lacks spots on the chest and belly.

Female: same as male

Juvenile: similar to winter plumage, with a darker bill

Nest: ground; male builds; 2 broods per year

Eggs: 3–4; brownish with brown markings

Incubation: 20–24 days; male incubates

Fledging: 17–21 days; male feeds the young

Migration: complete, to southern states, Mexico, and Central and South America

Food: aquatic insects

Compare: The Greater Yellowlegs (p. 161) is much larger. The Killdeer (p. 151) has 2 black neck bands. Look for the black spots on the chest and belly and the bobbing tail to help identify the breeding Spotted Sandpiper.

Stan's Notes: Seen along the shorelines of large ponds, lakes and rivers. One of the few shorebirds that will dive underwater when pursued. Able to fly straight up out of the water. Holds wings in a cup-like arc in flight, rarely lifting them above a horizontal plane. Walks as if delicately balanced. When standing, constantly bobs its tail. Gives a rapid series of "weet-weet-weet" calls when frightened and flying away. Female mates with multiple males and lays eggs in up to five nests. Male does all of the nest building, incubating and childcare without any help from the female.

female

male
p. 277

juvenile

Northern Cardinal
Cardinalis cardinalis

YEAR-ROUND

Size: 8–9" (20–23 cm)

Female: buff brown with a black mask, a large reddish bill and red tinges on the crest and wings

Male: red with a large crest and bill and a black mask extending from the face to the throat

Juvenile: same as female but with a blackish-gray bill

Nest: cup; female builds; 2–3 broods per year

Eggs: 3–4; bluish white with brown markings

Incubation: 12–13 days; female and male incubate

Fledging: 9–10 days; female and male feed the young

Migration: non-migrator

Food: seeds, insects, fruit; comes to seed feeders

Compare: The Cedar Waxwing (p. 129) has a small dark bill. The juvenile Northern Cardinal (bottom inset) looks like the adult female but with a dark bill. Look for the reddish bill to identify the female Northern Cardinal.

Stan's Notes: A familiar backyard bird. Seen in a variety of habitats, including parks. Usually likes thick vegetation. One of the few species in which both females and males sing. Can be heard all year. Listen for its "whata-cheer-cheer-cheer" territorial call in spring. Watch for a male feeding a female during courtship. The male also feeds the young of the first brood while the female builds a second nest. Territorial in spring, fighting its own reflection in a window or other reflective surface. Non-territorial in winter, gathering in small flocks of up to 20 birds. Makes short flights from cover to cover, often landing on the ground. *Cardinalis* denotes importance, as represented by the red priestly garments of Catholic cardinals.

male
p. 29

female

Red-winged Blackbird
Agelaius phoeniceus

YEAR-ROUND

Size:	8½" (21.5 cm)
Female:	heavily streaked brown with a pointed brown bill and white eyebrows
Male:	jet black with red-and-yellow shoulder patches (epaulets) and a pointed black bill
Juvenile:	same as female
Nest:	cup; female builds; 2–3 broods per year
Eggs:	3–4; bluish green with brown markings
Incubation:	10–12 days; female incubates
Fledging:	11–14 days; female and male feed the young
Migration:	non-migrator to partial; some will move to southern states, Mexico and Central America
Food:	seeds, insects; visits seed and suet feeders
Compare:	The female Rose-breasted Grosbeak (p. 133) is plumper and has a thicker bill. The female Brown-headed Cowbird (p. 127) lacks streaks. Look for white eyebrows and heavy streaking to identify the female Red-winged.

Stan's Notes: One of the most widespread and numerous birds in Ohio. Found around marshes, wetlands, lakes and rivers. It is a sure sign of spring when these birds return home. Flocks with as many as 10,000 birds have been reported. Males arrive before females and sing to defend their territory. The male repeats his call from the top of a cattail while showing off his red-and-yellow shoulder patches. The female chooses a mate and often builds her nest over shallow water in a thick stand of cattails. The male can be aggressive when defending the nest. Feeds mostly on seeds in spring and fall, and insects throughout the summer.

female

male

Common Nighthawk
Chordeiles minor

SUMMER

Size: 9" (23 cm)

Male: Camouflaged brown and white with a white chin. Distinctive white band across the wings and tail, seen only in flight.

Female: similar to male, with a tan chin; lacks a white tail band

Juvenile: similar to female

Nest: no nest; lays eggs on the ground, usually on rocks or a rooftop; 1 brood per year

Eggs: 2; cream with lavender markings

Incubation: 19–20 days; female and male incubate

Fledging: 20–21 days; female and male feed the young

Migration: complete, to South America

Food: insects caught in the air

Compare: The Chimney Swift (p. 93) is much smaller. Look for the obvious white band on the wings and characteristic flap-flap-flap-glide pattern to help identify the Common Nighthawk.

Stan's Notes: Usually only seen in flight at dusk or after sunset but not uncommon to see it sleeping on a branch during the day. A prolific insect eater and very noisy in flight, repeating a "peenting" call. Alternates slow wingbeats with bursts of quick wingbeats. In cities, prefers to nest on flat rooftops with gravel. City populations are on the decline as gravel rooftops are converted to other styles. In spring, the male performs a showy mating ritual consisting of a steep diving flight ending with a loud popping noise. One of the first birds to migrate in fall. Seen in large flocks, all heading south.

male

female

Northern Bobwhite
Colinus virginianus

YEAR-ROUND

Size: 10" (25 cm)

Male: Short, stocky and mostly brown with short gray tail. Prominent white eye stripe and white chin. Reddish-brown sides and belly, often with black lines and dots.

Female: similar to male, with buff-brown eye stripe and chin

Juvenile: smaller and duller than adults

Nest: ground; female and male construct; 1 brood per year

Eggs: 12–15; white to creamy without markings

Incubation: 23–24 days; female and male incubate

Fledging: 6–7 days; female and male feed the young

Migration: non-migrator

Food: insects, seeds, fruit; will come to ground feeders offering corn and millet

Compare: Much smaller than the female Ring-necked Pheasant (p. 199) and lacks the long tail.

Stan's Notes: Prefers shrubs, orchards, hedgerows and pastures. Moves around in small flocks of 20 birds (often family members), called a covey. The covey often rests together during the night, in a tight circle with tails together and heads facing outward, to watch for predators. Males and females perform distraction displays when nests or young are threatened. Nest is a depression in the ground lined with grass. Often pulls nearby vegetation over nest to help conceal it. Male gives a rising whistle, "bob-white," heard mainly in spring and summer. Also gives a single "hoy" call year-round.

in flight

juvenile

male

female

in-flight
juvenile

American Kestrel
Falco sparverius

Size: 9–11" (23–28 cm); up to 2' wingspan

Male: Rust-brown back and tail. White breast with dark spots. 2 vertical black lines on a white face. Blue-gray wings. Wide black band with a white edge on the tip of a rusty tail.

Female: similar to male but slightly larger, with rust-brown wings and dark bands on the tail

Juvenile: same as adult of the same sex

Nest: cavity; does not build a nest; 1 brood per year

Eggs: 4–5; white with brown markings

Incubation: 29–31 days; male and female incubate

Fledging: 30–31 days; female and male feed the young

Migration: non-migrator to partial in Ohio

Food: insects, small mammals and birds, reptiles

Compare: The Merlin (p. 149) is less common and lacks vertical black mustache marks. The Peregrine Falcon (p. 243) is much larger and has a dark "hood" marking. No other small bird of prey has a rusty back and tail.

YEAR-ROUND

Stan's Notes: An unusual raptor because the sexes look different (dimorphic). Due to its small size, this falcon was once called a Sparrow Hawk. Hovers near roads, then dives for prey. Watch for it to pump its tail after landing on a perch. Perches nearly upright. Eats many grasshoppers. Adapts quickly to a wooden nest box. Can be extremely vocal, giving a loud series of high-pitched calls. Ability to see ultraviolet (UV) light helps it locate mice and other prey by their urine, which glows bright yellow in UV light.

Lesser Yellowlegs

Tringa flavipes

MIGRATION

Size: 10–12" (25–30 cm)

Male: Typical sandpiper-type bird with a brown back and wings and a streaked white chest. Thin, straight, black bill. Long yellow legs.

Female: same as male

Juvenile: same as adults

Nest: ground; female builds; 1 brood per year

Eggs: 3–4; yellowish with brown markings

Incubation: 22–23 days; male and female incubate

Fledging: 18–20 days; male and female lead the young to food

Migration: complete, to southern coastal states, Mexico, and Central and South America

Food: aquatic insects, tiny fish

Compare: The Greater Yellowlegs (p. 161) is much larger and has a longer, slightly upturned bill. The breeding Spotted Sandpiper (p. 135) has black spots on its chest.

Stan's Notes: Often seen in small flocks, combing shorelines and mudflats in search of food. Usually walks with its head down and tail up, ready to snatch up prey. Uses its long, straight bill to pluck insects and tiny fish out of the water. A member of the sandpiper group known as Tattlers, which scream alarm calls when taking off. Quite often moves into the water before taking flight and gives a variety of flight notes at takeoff. Nest is a simple depression atop a mound of earth. Nests in marshes in the spruce forests of central Alaska and Canada. Migrates earlier than the Greater Yellowlegs in the fall and later in the spring.

male

in flight

female

juvenile

in-flight
juvenile

Merlin
Falco columbarius

Size: 10–12" (25–30 cm); up to 3' wingspan

Male: Dark back with a streaked chest. Rusty wash on the chest, undersides and leg feathers.

MIGRATION

Female: similar to male but slightly larger, with a light-brown back and head

Juvenile: similar to female

Nest: platform, or in a cavity on a cliff; female builds; 1 brood per year

Eggs: 4–7; white with rust-brown markings

Incubation: 28–32 days; male and female incubate

Fledging: 30–35 days; female and male feed the young

Migration: complete, to Gulf Coast states, Mexico, and Central and South America

Food: birds, insects, small mammals, reptiles

Compare: The American Kestrel (p. 145) is overall more rusty and has bold vertical, black mustache marks. The Peregrine Falcon (p. 243) is larger and has a dark "hood" head marking.

Stan's Notes: Once called a Pigeon Hawk. Feeds mostly on birds. In urban areas, seems to prefer House Finches. Catches most of its prey in flight, giving a burst of speed near the ground rather than diving or hovering like other falcons. Males return to the same breeding territory before females arrive. Defends territory against other raptors, including other Merlins. Sometimes young males help adult males defend their territory. During courtship, the male brings food to the female to demonstrate his ability to provide for her during incubation. Monogamous, with a long-term pair bond. Nests alone in tall conifers in woodlands and urban areas.

Killdeer

Charadrius vociferus

YEAR-ROUND SUMMER

Size:	11" (28 cm)
Male:	Upland shorebird with 2 black bands around the neck, like a necklace. Brown back and white belly. Bright reddish-orange rump, visible in flight.
Female:	same as male
Juvenile:	similar to adults, with a single neck band
Nest:	ground; male scrapes; 2 broods per year
Eggs:	3–5; tan with brown markings
Incubation:	24–28 days; male and female incubate
Fledging:	25 days; male and female lead their young to food
Migration:	complete, to southern Ohio, southern states, Mexico and Central America
Food:	insects, worms, snails
Compare:	The Spotted Sandpiper (p. 135) is found around water and lacks the 2 neck bands of the Killdeer.

Stan's Notes: Technically classified as a shorebird but lives in dry habitats instead of the shore. Often found in vacant fields, gravel pits, driveways, wetland edges or along railroad tracks. The only shorebird that has two black neck bands. Known to fake a broken wing to draw intruders away from the nest; once the nest is safe, the parent will take flight. Nests are just a slight depression in a dry area and are often hard to see. Hatchlings look like miniature adults walking on stilts. Soon after hatching, the young follow their parents around and peck for insects. Gives a loud and distinctive "kill-deer" call. Migrates in small flocks.

Brown Thrasher
Toxostoma rufum

YEAR-ROUND
SUMMER

Size: 11" (28 cm)

Male: Rust-red with a long tail. Heavy streaking on the breast and belly. 2 white wing bars. Long, curved bill and bright-yellow eyes.

Female: same as male

Juvenile: same as adults but with grayish eyes

Nest: cup; female and male build; 2 broods per year

Eggs: 4–5; pale blue with brown markings

Incubation: 11–14 days; female and male incubate

Fledging: 10–13 days; female and male feed the young

Migration: complete, to southern states; non-migrator in southern Ohio

Food: insects, fruit

Compare: The Fox Sparrow (p. 123) has a similar rust-red coloration, but the Thrasher is much larger, is thinner, and has a longer bill and tail. Look for the long rust-red tail to help identify the Brown Thrasher.

Stan's Notes: A prodigious songster. Sings along forest edges and in suburban yards. Often found in thick shrubs, where it will sing deliberate musical phrases, repeating each twice. The male Brown Thrasher has the largest documented repertoire of all North American songbirds, with more than 1,100 types of songs. Builds nest low in dense shrubs, often in fencerows. Quickly flies or runs on the ground in and out of thick shrubs. A noisy feeder due to its habit of turning over leaves, small rocks and branches to find food. More abundant in the central Great Plains than anywhere else in North America.

male

female

Northern Flicker

Colaptes auratus

YEAR-ROUND

Size: 12" (30 cm)

Male: Brown and black with a black mustache and black necklace. Red spot on the nape of the neck. Speckled chest. Large white rump patch, seen only when flying.

Female: same as male but without a black mustache

Juvenile: same as adult of the same sex

Nest: cavity; female and male excavate; 1 brood per year

Eggs: 5–8; white without markings

Incubation: 11–14 days; female and male incubate

Fledging: 25–28 days; female and male feed the young

Migration: non-migrator in Ohio; will move around during winter in search of food

Food: insects (especially ants and beetles); comes to suet feeders

Compare: The male Yellow-bellied Sapsucker (p. 51) has a red chin. The male Red-bellied Woodpecker (p. 57) has a red crown. Flickers are the only brown-backed woodpeckers in Ohio.

Stan's Notes: This is the only woodpecker to regularly feed on the ground. Prefers ants and beetles and produces an antacid saliva that neutralizes the acidic defense of ants. The male often picks the nest site. Parents take up to 12 days to excavate the cavity. Can be attracted to your yard with a nest box stuffed with sawdust. Often reuses an old nest. Undulates deeply during flight, flashing yellow under its wings and tail and calling "wacka-wacka" loudly.

Mourning Dove
Zenaida macroura

YEAR-ROUND

Size: 12" (30 cm)

Male: Smooth and fawn-colored. Gray patch on the head. Iridescent pink and greenish blue on the neck. Black spot behind and below the eyes. Black spots on the wings and tail. Pointed, wedged tail; white edges seen in flight.

Female: similar to male, but lacks the pink-and-green iridescent neck feathers

Juvenile: spotted and streaked plumage

Nest: platform; female and male build; 2 broods per year

Eggs: 2; white without markings

Incubation: 13–14 days; male incubates during the day, female incubates at night

Fledging: 12–14 days; female and male feed the young

Migration: non-migrator to partial; moves around the state to find food

Food: seeds; will visit ground and seed feeders

Compare: Lacks the wide range of color combinations of the Rock Pigeon (p. 239). Lacks the black collar of the Eurasian Collared-Dove (p. 237).

Stan's Notes: Name comes from its mournful cooing. A ground feeder, bobbing its head as it walks. One of the few birds to drink without lifting its head, like the Rock Pigeon. The parents feed the young (squab) a regurgitated liquid called crop-milk during their first few days of life. Platform nest is so flimsy it often falls apart in a storm. During takeoff and in flight, wind rushes through the bird's wing feathers, creating a characteristic whistling sound.

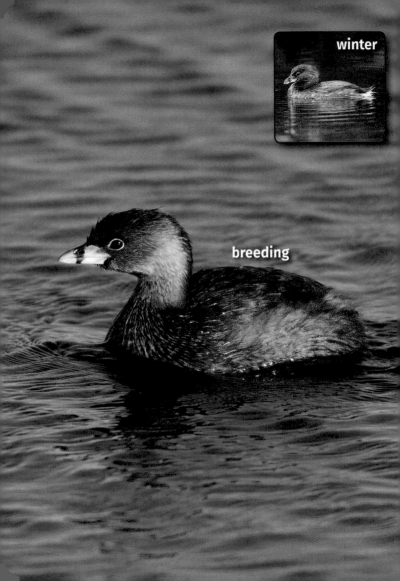

winter

breeding

Pied-billed Grebe
Podilymbus podiceps

YEAR-ROUND
SUMMER

Size: 12–14" (30–36 cm)

Male: Small and brown with a black chin and fluffy white patch beneath the tail. Black ring around a thick, chicken-like, ivory bill. Winter bill is brown and unmarked.

Female: same as male

Juvenile: paler than adults, with white spots and a gray chest, belly and bill

Nest: floating platform; female and male construct; 1 brood per year

Eggs: 5–7; bluish white without markings

Incubation: 22–24 days; female and male incubate

Fledging: 45–60 days; female and male feed the young

Migration: partial, to southern Ohio, where it finds open water; southern states; Mexico

Food: crayfish, aquatic insects, fish

Compare: Look for the white patch under the tail and the thick bill to help identify the Pied-billed.

Stan's Notes: A summer waterbird in the state, often seen diving for food. When disturbed, it slowly sinks like a submarine, quickly compressing its feathers, forcing the air out. Was called Hell-diver due to the length of time it can stay submerged. Able to surface far from where it went under. Well suited to life on water, with short wings, lobed toes, and legs set close to the rear of its body. Swims easily but moves awkwardly on land. Very sensitive to pollution. Builds nest on a floating mat in water. "Grebe" may originate from the Breton word *krib*, meaning "crest," referring to the crested head plumes of many grebes, especially during breeding season.

Greater Yellowlegs
Tringa melanoleuca

MIGRATION

Size: 13–15" (33–38 cm)

Male: Tall with a bulbous head and a long, thin, slightly upturned bill. Gray streaking on the chest. White belly. Long yellow legs.

Female: same as male

Juvenile: same as adults

Nest: ground; female builds; 1 brood per year

Eggs: 3–4; off-white with brown markings

Incubation: 22–23 days; female and male incubate

Fledging: 18–20 days; male and female feed the young

Migration: complete, to southern states, Mexico, and Central and South America

Food: small fish, aquatic insects

Compare: The Lesser Yellowlegs (p. 147) is much smaller and has a shorter bill. The Killdeer (p. 151) has 2 black bands around its neck. The breeding Spotted Sandpiper (p. 135) has spots on its chest. Look for the long yellow legs and long bill to identify the Greater Yellowlegs.

Stan's Notes: A common shorebird, often seen during migration. Can be identified by its long legs, which enable it to wade in deep water, and its slightly upturned bill. Often seen resting on one leg. Rushes forward through the water to feed, plowing its bill or swinging it from side to side, catching small fish and insects. A skittish bird, it is quick to give an alarm call, causing flocks to take flight. Typically moves into the water before taking flight. Gives a variety of "flight" notes at takeoff. Nests on the ground close to water on the northern tundra of Labrador and Newfoundland.

male

female

Green-winged Teal

Anas crecca

MIGRATION WINTER

Size: 14–15" (36–38 cm)

Male: Chestnut head with a dark-green patch out-lined with white from the eyes to the nape of the neck. Gray body. Butter-yellow tail. Green patch on the wings (speculum), seen in flight.

Female: light brown with black spots and a green speculum; small bill

Juvenile: same as female

Nest: ground; female builds; 1 brood per year

Eggs: 8–10; cream white without markings

Incubation: 21–23 days; female incubates

Fledging: 32–34 days; female teaches the young to feed

Migration: complete to northern Ohio; moves around to find open water

Food: aquatic plants and insects

Compare: The female Blue-winged Teal (p. 165) is simi-lar in size, but it has slight white at the base of its bill. Look for the chestnut head with a dark-green patch on each side to identify the male Green-winged Teal.

Stan's Notes: One of the smallest dabbling ducks. Tips forward in water to feed off the bottom of shallow ponds. This behavior makes it vulnerable to ingesting spent lead shot, which can cause death. It walks well on land and will also feed in flooded fields and woodlands. Known for its fast and agile flight. Groups wheel and spin through the air in tight formation. The green wing patches are most obvious during flight.

male

female

Blue-winged Teal
Spatula discors

SUMMER MIGRATION

Size: 15–16" (38–41 cm)

Male: Small, plain-looking brown duck with black speckles and a large, crescent-shaped white mark at the base of the bill. Gray head. Black tail with a small white patch. Blue wing patch (speculum), best seen in flight.

Female: duller than male, with only slight white at the base of the bill; lacks a crescent mark on the face and a white patch on the tail

Juvenile: same as female

Nest: ground; female builds; 1 brood per year

Eggs: 8–11; cream white

Incubation: 23–27 days; female incubates

Fledging: 35–44 days; female feeds the young

Migration: complete, to southern states, Mexico and Central America

Food: aquatic plants, seeds, aquatic insects

Compare: Female Green-winged Teal (p. 163) lacks white near its bill. The female Mallard (p. 189) has an orange-and-black bill. The female Wood Duck (p. 179) has a crest. Look for the white facial mark to identify the male Blue-winged.

Stan's Notes: Migrates farther than most other ducks. Nesting is widespread, as far north as Alaska. Constructs nest some distance from the water. Female performs a distraction display to protect the nest and young. Male leaves the female near the end of incubation. Planting crops and cultivating to pond edges have caused declining populations.

165

soaring

Red-shouldered Hawk

Buteo lineatus

YEAR-ROUND

Size:	15–19" (38–48 cm); up to 3½' wingspan
Male:	Reddish (cinnamon) head, shoulders, breast and belly. Wings and back are dark brown with white spots. Long tail with thin white bands and wide black bands. Obvious red wing linings, seen in flight.
Female:	same as male
Juvenile:	similar to adults but lacks the cinnamon color; white chest with dark spots
Nest:	platform; female and male construct; 1 brood per year
Eggs:	2-4; white with dark markings
Incubation:	27-29 days; female and male incubate
Fledging:	39-45 days; female feeds the young
Migration:	non-migrator to partial in Ohio; moves around to find food
Food:	reptiles, amphibians, large insects, birds
Compare:	The Red-tailed Hawk (p. 193) has a white chest. The Sharp-shinned Hawk (p. 235) is smaller and lacks the reddish head and belly of the Red-shouldered Hawk.

Stan's Notes: Common woodland hawk in Ohio. Seen in backyards. Likes to hunt at forest edges, spotting snakes, frogs, insects, occasional small birds and other prey as it perches. Often flaps with an alternating gliding pattern. Very vocal with a distinct scream. Breeds when it reaches 2–3 years. Remains in the same territory for many years. Starts constructing its nest in March or April. Young leave the nest in June or July.

male p. 59

female

Lesser Scaup
Aythya affinis

MIGRATION
WINTER

Size:	16–17" (40–43 cm)
Female:	Overall brown duck with a dull white patch at the base of a light-gray bill. Yellow eyes.
Male:	White and gray; the chest and head appear nearly black but the head looks purple with green highlights in direct sun. Yellow eyes.
Juvenile:	same as female
Nest:	ground; female builds; 1 brood per year
Eggs:	8–14; olive buff without markings
Incubation:	22–28 days; female incubates
Fledging:	45–50 days; female teaches young to feed
Migration:	complete, to northern Ohio along Lake Erie; moves around to find open water and food
Food:	aquatic plants and insects
Compare:	The male Blue-winged Teal (p. 165) is slightly smaller and has a crescent-shaped white mark at the base of its bill.

Stan's Notes: A common diving duck. Often seen in large flocks on lakes, ponds and sewage lagoons. Submerges itself completely to feed on the bottom of lakes (unlike dabbling ducks, which only tip forward to reach the bottom). Note the bold white stripe under the wings when in flight. The male leaves the female when she starts incubating eggs. The quantity of eggs (clutch size) increases with the age of the female. This species has an interesting babysitting arrangement in which groups of young (crèches) are tended by one to three adult females.

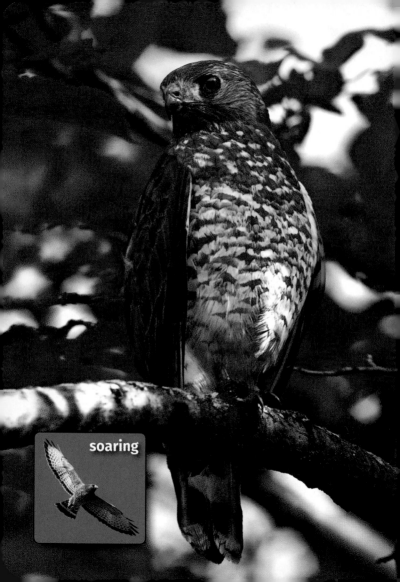

soaring

Broad-winged Hawk
Buteo platypterus

SUMMER

Size: 14–19" (36–48 cm); up to 3' wingspan

Male: Brown back and rust-red bars on the breast. 2 or 3 wide black-and-white tail bands. Short, round wings. White under the wings and black "fingertips," seen in flight.

Female: same as male but slightly larger

Juvenile: tail bands narrower and more numerous; brown-streaked chest and belly

Nest: platform; female and male build, but female finishes; 1 brood per year

Eggs: 2–3; off-white with brown markings

Incubation: 28–32 days; female incubates; male feeds the female during incubation

Fledging: 34–40 days; female and male feed the young

Migration: complete, to Central and South America

Food: small birds, small mammals, snakes, frogs, toads, large insects

Compare: Cooper's Hawk (p. 241) has a longer, thinner tail. The Sharp-shinned Hawk (p. 235) is much smaller. Look for the black-and-white tail bands to identify the Broad-winged.

Stan's Notes: A common woodland hawk in Ohio. Seen in large groups (kettles) migrating in early fall. Spends most of its time hunting small birds, snakes and frogs in dense woods. Short wings help it navigate around trees. Often heard before it is seen. Screams a high-pitched whistle call repetitively when intruders are near the nest. Performs a sky-dance courtship with steep dives, sharp flights upward and rolling over. Very vocal during courtship.

Barn Owl
Tyto alba

YEAR-ROUND SUMMER

Size: 16–19" (40–48 cm); up to 4' wingspan

Male: "Non-eared" owl with a rusty-brown back of head, back, wings and tail. Heart-shaped white face, outlined in darker rusty brown. White chest and belly. Dark eyes. Long gray legs. Gray feet. Yellow bill.

Female: similar to male, often with a rusty wash over the chest and belly

Juvenile: light gray to white; fuzzy-looking overall

Nest: cavity, occasionally on a cliff crevice; female builds; 1 brood per year

Eggs: 3–7; white without markings

Incubation: 30–34 days; female incubates

Fledging: 52–56 days; male and female feed the young

Migration: non-migrator to complete

Food: small mammals, birds, snakes

Compare: The Eastern Screech-Owl (p. 227) is smaller, has ear tufts and lacks the white face of the Barn Owl.

Stan's Notes: This owl is well known for nesting in old barns (hence the common name) but will also nest in any dark cavity on cliffs or in trees. The male feeds the female during incubation. Clutch size depends on the availability of prey: the more prey, the larger the clutch. Young hatch one per day (asynchronously) over two weeks, creating a range of ages in the nest. Will sway back and forth with lowered head when confronted.

male
p. 61

female

Hooded Merganser
Lophodytes cucullatus

YEAR-ROUND

Size: 16–19" (41–48 cm)

Female: Sleek brown-and-rust bird with a red head. Ragged "hair" on the back of the head. Long, thin, brown bill.

Male: black back, rust-brown sides, long black bill; raises crest "hood" to display a white patch

Juvenile: similar to female

Nest: cavity; female lines an old woodpecker cavity or a nest box near water; 1 brood per year

Eggs: 10–12; white without markings

Incubation: 32–33 days; female incubates

Fledging: 71 days; female feeds the young

Migration: non-migrator to partial, to southern states; moves around in winter to find open water and food

Food: small fish, aquatic insects, crustaceans (especially crayfish)

Compare: The female Common Merganser (p. 281) is much larger and has a white chin and orange bill. Look for the ragged "hair" on the back of the head to help identify the female Hoodie.

Stan's Notes: A small diving duck, found in shallow ponds, sloughs, lakes and rivers. Usually in small groups. Quick, low flight across the water, with fast wingbeats. Male has a deep, rolling call. Female gives a hoarse quack. Nests in wooded areas. Female will lay some eggs in the nests of other mergansers, goldeneyes or Wood Ducks (egg dumping), resulting in 20–25 eggs in some nests. Rarely, she shares a nest, sitting with a Wood Duck.

male p. 63

female

Ring-necked Duck
Aythya collaris

**MIGRATION
WINTER**

Size:	16–19" (41–48 cm)
Female:	Brown with a darker brown back and crown and lighter-brown sides. Gray face. White eye-ring with a white line behind the eye. White ring around the bill. Peaked head.
Male:	Black head, chest and back. Gray to white sides. Blue bill with a bold white ring and a thinner ring at the base. Peaked head.
Juvenile:	similar to female
Nest:	ground; female builds; 1 brood per year
Eggs:	8–10; olive to brown without markings
Incubation:	26–27 days; female incubates
Fledging:	49–56 days; female teaches the young to feed
Migration:	complete, to southern Ohio and southern states
Food:	aquatic plants and insects
Compare:	The female Lesser Scaup (p. 169) is similar in size. Look for the white ring around the bill to help identify the female Ring-necked Duck.

Stan's Notes: Often seen in larger freshwater lakes, usually in small flocks or just pairs. A diving duck, watch for it to dive underwater to forage for food. Springs up off the water to take flight. Has a distinctive tall, peaked head with a sloped forehead. Flattens its crown when diving. Male gives a quick series of grating barks and grunts. Female gives high-pitched peeps. Named "Ring-necked" for its cinnamon collar, which is nearly impossible to see in the field. Also called Ring-billed Duck due to the white ring on its bill.

male
p. 255

female

SUMMER

Wood Duck
Aix sponsa

Size: 17–20" (43–51 cm)

Female: Small brown dabbling duck. Bright-white eye-ring and a not-so-obvious crest. Blue patch on wings (speculum), often hidden.

Male: highly ornamented, with a mostly green head and crest patterned with black and white; rusty chest, white belly and red eyes

Juvenile: similar to female

Nest: cavity; female lines an old woodpecker cavity or a nest box in a tree; 1 brood per year

Eggs: 10–15; cream white without markings

Incubation: 28–36 days; female incubates

Fledging: 56–68 days; female teaches the young to feed

Migration: complete, to southern states

Food: aquatic insects, plants, seeds

Compare: The female Mallard (p. 189) and female Blue-winged Teal (p. 165) lack the eye-ring and crest. The female Northern Shoveler (p. 191) has a large, spoon-shaped bill.

Stan's Notes: A common duck of quiet, shallow backwater ponds. Nearly went extinct around 1900 due to overhunting, but it's doing well now. Nests in a tree cavity or a nest box in a tree. Seen flying in forests or perching on high branches. Female takes off with a loud, squealing call and enters the nest cavity from full flight. Lays some eggs in a neighboring nest (egg dumping), resulting in more than 20 eggs in some clutches. Hatchlings stay in the nest for 24 hours, then jump from as high as 60 feet (18 m) to the ground or water to follow their mother. They never return to the nest.

female

male
p. 65

WINTER

Common Goldeneye
Bucephala clangula

Size: 18–20" (45–51 cm)

Female: Brown and gray duck with a large dark-brown head and gray body. White collar. Bright-golden eyes. Yellow-tipped dark bill.

Male: mostly white with a black back, a puffy green head, a large white spot on the face, bright-golden eyes and a dark bill

Juvenile: same as female but with a dark bill

Nest: cavity; female lines an old woodpecker cavity; 1 brood per year

Eggs: 8–10; light green without markings

Incubation: 28–32 days; female incubates

Fledging: 56–59 days; female leads the young to food

Migration: complete, to Ohio, southern states and Mexico

Food: aquatic plants, insects, fish, mollusks

Compare: Similar to female Lesser Scaup (p. 169), which is smaller. Look for the dark-brown head, white collar and golden-yellow eye to help identify the female Common Goldeneye.

Stan's Notes: Known for the loud whistling sound produced by its wings during flight. During late winter and early spring, the male performs elaborate mating displays that include throwing his head back and calling a raspy note. Female will lay some of her eggs in other goldeneye nests or in the nests of other species (egg dumping), causing some mothers to incubate as many as 30 eggs in a brood. Named for its bright-golden eyes.

female

male
p. 245

soaring

Northern Harrier
Circus hudsonius

YEAR-ROUND

Size: 18–22" (45–56 cm); up to 4-ft. wingspan

Female: Slender, low-flying hawk with a dark-brown back and brown streaking on the chest and belly. Large white rump patch. Thin black tail bands and black wing tips. Yellow eyes.

Male: silver gray with a large white rump patch and white belly; faint, thin bands across tail; black wing tips; and yellow eyes

Juvenile: similar to female, with an orange chest

Nest: ground; female and male construct; 1 brood per year

Eggs: 4–8; bluish white without markings

Incubation: 31–32 days; female incubates

Fledging: 30–35 days; male and female feed the young

Migration: non-migrator to partial in Ohio; moves around to find food

Food: mice, snakes, insects, small birds

Compare: Slimmer than the Red-tailed Hawk (p. 193). Look for the characteristic low gliding and the black tail bands to identify the female Harrier.

Stan's Notes: One of the easiest of hawks to identify. Glides just above the ground, following the contours of the land while searching for prey. Holds its wings just above horizontal, tilting back and forth in the wind, similar to the Turkey Vulture. Formerly called Marsh Hawk due to its habit of hunting over marshes. Feeds and nests on the ground. Will also preen and rest on the ground. Unlike other hawks, mainly uses its hearing to find prey, followed by its sight. At any age, it has a distinctive owl-like face disk.

dark morph

light morph

soaring dark morph

soaring light morph

Rough-legged Hawk
Buteo lagopus

WINTER

Size: 18–23" (45–58 cm); up to 4½' wingspan

Male: 2 color morphs, both with distinctive dark "wrists." Dark belly, long white tail and dark tail band. Feathered legs, small yellow feet. Small bill. Light morph has a white trailing edge on the wings. Dark morph is brown with a light-gray trailing edge on the wings.

Female: same as male but slightly larger

Juvenile: same as adults

Nest: platform on the edge of a cliff; female and male build; 1 brood per year

Eggs: 2–6; white without markings

Incubation: 28–31 days; female and male incubate

Fledging: 39–43 days; female and male feed the young

Migration: complete, to Ohio and the northern half of the U.S.; migrates from Canada and Alaska

Food: small mammals, snakes, large insects

Compare: The Red-tailed Hawk (p. 193) has a belly band and lacks dark "wrist" marks. The Osprey (p. 69) has similar dark "wrists" but lacks the dark belly of the Rough-legged Hawk.

Stan's Notes: The light morph is more common than the dark, but both are seen together in groups of 10–25 birds. A common winter resident, more numerous in some years than in others. It has much smaller, weaker feet than other raptors and must hunt for smaller prey. Hunts in flight over fields, often hovering before diving for a mouse or a vole. Also watches for prey from a perch. Feeds on the ground. Monogamous, with long-term pair bonds.

male p. 279

female

Redhead
Aythya americana

Size: 19" (48 cm)

Female: Soft-brown, plain-looking duck with gray to white wing linings. Rounded top of head. Two-toned bill, gray with a black tip.

Male: Rich-red head and neck with a black chest and tail, gray sides, and smoky-gray wings and back. Tricolored bill with a light-blue base, white ring and black tip.

Juvenile: similar to female

Nest: cup; female builds; 1 brood per year

Eggs: 9-14; pale white without markings

Incubation: 24-28 days; female and male incubate

Fledging: 56-73 days; female shows young what to eat

Migration: complete, to northern Ohio and southern states; moves around to find open water and food

Food: seeds, aquatic plants, insects

Compare: The female Northern Shoveler (p. 191) is lighter brown with an exceptionally large, shovel-shaped bill.

Stan's Notes: A duck of permanent large bodies of water. Forages along the shoreline, feeding on seeds, aquatic plants and insects. Usually builds nest directly on the water's surface, using large mats of vegetation. Female lays up to 75 percent of its eggs in the nests of other Redheads and several other duck species. Overall populations seem to be increasing at about 2–3 percent each year.

male
p. 259

female

Mallard
Anas platyrhynchos

YEAR-ROUND

Size:	19–21" (48–53 cm)
Female:	brown duck with an orange-and-black bill and blue-and-white wing mark (speculum)
Male:	large green head, white necklace, rust-brown or chestnut chest, combination of gray-and-white sides, yellow bill, orange legs and feet
Juvenile:	same as female but with a yellow bill
Nest:	ground; female builds; 1 brood per year
Eggs:	7–10; greenish to whitish, unmarked
Incubation:	26–30 days; female incubates
Fledging:	42–52 days; female leads the young to food
Migration:	non-migrator in Ohio; moves around to find food
Food:	seeds, plants, aquatic insects; will come to ground feeders offering corn
Compare:	The female Northern Shoveler (p. 191) is smaller and has a large, spoon-shaped bill. The female Wood Duck (p. 179) has a white eye-ring. The female Blue-winged Teal (p. 165) is smaller than the female Mallard.

Stan's Notes: A familiar dabbling duck of lakes and ponds. Also found in rivers, streams and some backyards. Tips forward to feed on vegetation on the bottom of shallow water. The name "Mallard" comes from the Latin word *masculus,* meaning "male," referring to the male's habit of taking no part in raising the young. Female and male have white underwings and white tails, but only the male has black central tail feathers that curl upward. The female gives a classic quack. Returns to its birthplace each year.

male
p. 261

female

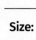

Northern Shoveler
Anas clypeata

SUMMER
MIGRATION

Size:	19–21" (48–53 cm)
Female:	Medium-size brown duck speckled with black. Green patch on the wings (speculum). Extraordinarily large, spoon-shaped bill.
Male:	iridescent green head, rusty sides, white chest, large spoon-shaped bill
Juvenile:	same as female
Nest:	ground; female builds; 1 brood per year
Eggs:	9–12; olive without markings
Incubation:	22–25 days; female incubates
Fledging:	30–60 days; female leads the young to food
Migration:	complete, to southern states, Mexico and Central America
Food:	aquatic insects, plants
Compare:	The female Wood Duck (p. 179) is smaller and has a white eye-ring. The female Mallard (p. 189) lacks the large bill. Look for the spoon-shaped bill to identify the Shoveler.

Stan's Notes: One of several species of shovelers. Called "Shoveler" due to the peculiar, shovel-like shape of its bill. Given the common name "Northern" because it is the only species of these ducks in North America. Seen in shallow wetlands, ponds and small lakes in flocks of 5–10 birds. Flocks fly in tight formation. Swims low in water, pointing its large bill toward the water as if it's too heavy to lift. Usually swims in tight circles while feeding. Feeds mainly by filtering tiny aquatic insects and plants from the surface of the water with its bill. Female gathers plant material and forms it into a nest a short distance from the water.

soaring

juvenile
soaring

juvenile

Red-tailed Hawk

Buteo jamaicensis

YEAR-ROUND

Size: 19–23" (48–58 cm); up to 4½' wingspan

Male: Variety of colorations, from chocolate brown to nearly all white. Often brown with a white breast and brown belly band. Rust-red tail. Underside of wing is white with a small dark patch on the leading edge near the shoulder.

Female: same as male but slightly larger

Juvenile: similar to adults, with a speckled breast and light eyes; lacks a red tail

Nest: platform; male and female construct; 1 brood per year

Eggs: 2–3; white without markings, sometimes marked with brown

Incubation: 30–35 days; female and male incubate

Fledging: 45–46 days; male and female feed the young

Migration: non-migrator to partial in Ohio

Food: small and medium-size animals, large birds, snakes, fish, insects, bats, carrion

Compare: The female Northern Harrier (p. 183) is slimmer and lacks the red tail.

Stan's Notes: Common in open country and cities. Seen perching on fences, freeway lampposts and trees. Look for it circling above open fields and roadsides, searching for prey. Gives a high-pitched scream that trails off. Often builds a large stick nest in large trees along roads. Lines nest with finer material, like evergreen needles. Returns to the same nest site each year. The red tail develops in the second year and is best seen from above.

Barred Owl
Strix varia

Size: 20–24" (51–61 cm); up to 3½' wingspan

Male: Chunky brown-and-gray owl with a large head and dark-brown eyes. Dark horizontal barring on upper chest. Vertical streaks on lower chest and belly. Yellow bill and feet.

YEAR-ROUND

Female: same as male but slightly larger

Juvenile: light gray with a black face

Nest: cavity; does not add nesting material; 1 brood per year

Eggs: 2–3; white without markings

Incubation: 28–33 days; female incubates

Fledging: 42–44 days; female and male feed the young

Migration: non-migrator

Food: mice, rabbits and other animals; small birds; fish; reptiles; amphibians

Compare: Lacks the "horns" of the Great Horned Owl (p. 197) and the "ears" of the much smaller Eastern Screech-Owl (p. 227). Look for a stocky owl with a large head and dark-brown eyes to identify the Barred Owl.

Stan's Notes: A very common owl in the state. Prefers deciduous, dense woodlands with sparse undergrowth, but it can be attracted to your yard with a simple nest box that has a large entrance hole. Often seen hunting during the day. Perches and watches for mice, birds and other prey. Hovers over water and reaches down to grab fish. After fledging, the young stay with their parents for up to four months. Often sounds like a dog barking just before calling six to eight hoots, sounding like "who-who-who-cooks-for-you."

Great Horned Owl
Bubo virginianus

YEAR-ROUND

Size: 21–25" (53–64 cm); up to 4' wingspan

Male: Robust brown "horned" owl. Bright-yellow eyes and a V-shaped white throat resembling a necklace. Horizontal barring on the chest.

Female: same as male but slightly larger

Juvenile: similar to adults but lacks ear tufts

Nest: no nest; takes over the nest of a crow, hawk or Great Blue Heron or uses a partial cavity, stump or broken tree; 1 brood per year

Eggs: 2–3; white without markings

Incubation: 26–30 days; female incubates

Fledging: 30–35 days; male and female feed the young

Migration: non-migrator

Food: mammals, birds (ducks), snakes, insects

Compare: The Barred Owl (p. 195) has dark eyes and no "horns." The Eastern Screech-Owl (p. 227) is extremely tiny. Look for bright-yellow eyes and feather "horns" on the head to help identify the Great Horned Owl.

Stan's Notes: One of the earliest-nesting birds in Ohio, laying eggs in January and February. Can hear a mouse move beneath a foot of snow. The "horns," or "ears," are tufts of feathers and have nothing to do with hearing. Cannot turn its head all the way around. Wing feathers are ragged on the ends, resulting in silent flight. Eyelids close from the top down, like ours. Fearless, it is one of the few animals that will kill skunks and porcupines. Given that, it is also called the Flying Tiger. Call sounds like "hoo-hoo-hoo-hoooo."

male

female

Ring-necked Pheasant
Phasianus colchicus

Size: 30–36" (76–91 cm), male, including tail
21–25" (53–64 cm), female, including tail

Male: Golden-brown body with a long tail. White ring around the neck. Head is purple, green, blue and red.

Female: smaller and less flamboyant than the male, with brown plumage and a long tail

Juvenile: similar to female, with a shorter tail

Nest: ground; female builds; 1 brood per year

Eggs: 8–10; olive brown without markings

Incubation: 23–25 days; female incubates

Fledging: 11–12 days; female leads the young to food

Migration: non-migrator

Food: insects, seeds, fruit; visits ground feeders

Compare: Both male and female Ring-necked Pheasants have long tails, but the male is much larger and brightly colored.

Stan's Notes: Originally introduced to North America from China in the late 1800s. Common now throughout the U.S. Like many other game birds, its numbers vary greatly, making it common in some years, scarce in others. Seeks shelter during harsh winter weather. To attract females, the male gives a cackling call and then rapidly flutters his wings. Usually walks or runs. Takes off in an explosive flight with fast wingbeats followed by gliding low to the ground. Roosts on the ground or in trees at night. The name "Ring-necked" refers to the white ring around the male's neck. "Pheasant" comes from the Greek word *phaisianos*, which means "bird of the River Phasis" (known today as the Rioni River).

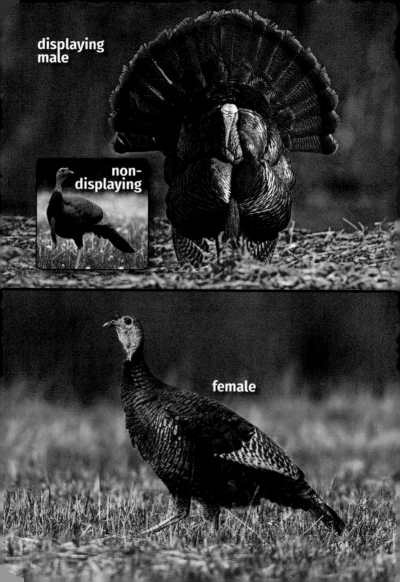

displaying male

non-displaying

female

Wild Turkey
Meleagris gallopavo

YEAR-ROUND

Size: 36–48" (91–122 cm)

Male: Large brown-and-bronze bird with a naked blue-and-red head. Long, straight, black beard in the center of the chest. Tail spreads open like a fan. Spurs on legs.

Female: thinner and less striking than the male; often lacks a breast beard

Juvenile: same as adult of the same sex

Nest: ground; female builds; 1 brood per year

Eggs: 10–12; buff white with dull-brown markings

Incubation: 27–28 days; female incubates

Fledging: 6–10 days; female leads the young to food

Migration: non-migrator; moves around to find food

Food: insects, seeds, fruit

Compare: This bird is quite distinctive and unlikely to be confused with any other.

Stan's Notes: The largest native game bird in Ohio, and the species from which the domestic turkey was bred. A strong flier that can approach 60 mph (97 kph). Can fly straight up, then away. Eyesight is three times better than ours. Hearing is also excellent; can hear competing males up to a mile away. Male has a "harem" of up to 20 females. Female scrapes out a shallow depression for nesting and pads it with soft leaves. Males are known as toms, females are hens, and young are poults. Roosts in trees at night. Eliminated from Ohio by the turn of the 20th century due to market hunting and loss of habitat, and reintroduced in the 1950–60s. Populations are now stable.

Ruby-crowned Kinglet
Regulus calendula

MIGRATION

Size: 4" (10 cm)

Male: Small, teardrop-shaped green to gray bird. 2 white wing bars and a white eye-ring. Hidden ruby crown.

Female: same as male, but lacks a ruby crown

Juvenile: same as female

Nest: pendulous; female builds; 1 brood per year

Eggs: 4–5; white with brown markings

Incubation: 11–12 days; female incubates

Fledging: 11–12 days; female and male feed the young

Migration: complete, to southern states, Mexico and Central America

Food: insects, berries

Compare: The female American Goldfinch (p. 293) shares the drab olive plumage and unmarked chest, but it is larger. Look for the white eye-ring to identify the Ruby-crowned Kinglet.

Stan's Notes: This is the second-smallest bird in Ohio. Most commonly seen during migration, when groups travel together. Watch for it flitting in thick shrubs low to the ground. It takes a quick eye to see the ruby crown, which the male flashes when he is excited. The female weaves an unusually intricate nest and fastens colorful lichens and mosses to the exterior with spiderwebs. Often builds the nest high in a mature tree, where it hangs from a branch that has overlapping leaves. Sings a distinctive song that starts out soft and ends loud and on a higher note. "Kinglet" originates from the word *king*, referring to the male's red crown, and the diminutive suffix *let*, meaning "small."

male

female

Golden-crowned Kinglet
Regulus satrapa

WINTER

Size: 4" (10 cm)

Male: Tiny, plump green to gray bird. Distinctive yellow-and-orange patch with a black border on the crown (top inset). White eyebrow mark. 2 white wing bars.

Female: same as male, but has a yellow crown with a black border, lacks any orange (bottom inset)

Juvenile: same as adults, but lacks gold on crown

Nest: pendulous; female builds; 1–2 broods per year

Eggs: 5–9; white or creamy with brown markings

Incubation: 14–15 days; female incubates

Fledging: 14–19 days; female and male feed the young

Migration: complete, to Ohio, southern states, Mexico and Central America

Food: insects, fruit, tree sap

Compare: Similar to the Ruby-crowned Kinglet (p. 203), but the Golden-crowned has an obvious crown. Smaller than the female American Goldfinch (p. 293), which has an all-black forehead.

Stan's Notes: Nests and raises young in the coniferous forests of Canada. Often seen in flocks with chickadees, nuthatches, woodpeckers and Ruby-crowned Kinglets. Flicks its wings when moving around. Constructs an unusual hanging nest, often with moss, lichens and spiderwebs, and lines it with bark and feathers. Can have so many eggs in its small nest that eggs are in two layers. Drinks tree sap and feeds by gleaning insects from trees. Can be very tame and approachable.

Red-breasted Nuthatch
Sitta canadensis

WINTER

Size: 4½" (11 cm)

Male: Gray-backed bird with an obvious black eye line and black cap. Rust-red breast and belly.

Female: duller than male and has a gray cap and pale undersides

Juvenile: same as female

Nest: cavity; male and female excavate a cavity or move into a vacant hole; 1 brood per year

Eggs: 5–6; white with red-brown markings

Incubation: 11–12 days; female incubates

Fledging: 14–20 days; female and male feed the young

Migration: irruptive; moves around in search of food

Food: insects, insect eggs, seeds; comes to seed and suet feeders

Compare: The White-breasted Nuthatch (p. 213) is larger and has a white breast. Look for the rust-red breast and black eye line to help identify the Red-breasted Nuthatch.

Stan's Notes: The nuthatch climbs down trunks of trees headfirst, searching for insects. Like a chickadee, it grabs a seed from a feeder and flies off to crack it open. Wedges the seed into a crevice and pounds it open with several sharp blows. The name "Nuthatch" comes from the Middle English moniker *nuthak*, referring to the habit of hacking seeds open. Look for it in mature conifers, where it extracts seeds from pine cones. Excavates a cavity or takes an old woodpecker hole or a natural cavity and builds a nest within. An irruptive migrator, common in some winters and scarce in others. Gives a series of nasal "yank-yank-yank" calls.

Black-capped Chickadee
Poecile atricapillus

YEAR-ROUND
WINTER

Size: 5" (13 cm)

Male: Familiar gray bird with a black cap and throat patch. Tan sides and belly. White chest. Small white wing marks.

Female: same as male

Juvenile: same as adults

Nest: cavity; female and male excavate or use a nest box; 1 brood per year

Eggs: 5–7; white with fine brown markings

Incubation: 11–13 days; female and male incubate

Fledging: 14–18 days; female and male feed the young

Migration: non-migrator to partial; moves around the state to find food

Food: seeds, insects, fruit; will come to seed and suet feeders

Compare: Identical to the Carolina Chickadee (p. 211), except in song: the Carolina's is a higher, faster version. The Tufted Titmouse (p. 219) is larger and has a crest.

Stan's Notes: A perky backyard bird that can be attracted with a nest box or bird feeder. Usually the first to find a new seed or suet feeder. Can be tamed and hand fed. Much of the diet comes from feeders, so it can be a common urban bird. Needs to feed every day in winter; forages even during the worst winter storms. Typically seen with nuthatches, woodpeckers and other birds. Builds nest mostly with green moss, lined with fur. Named for its familiar "chika-dee-dee-dee-dee" call. Also gives a high-pitched, two-toned "fee-bee" call. Can have different calls in different regions.

Carolina Chickadee
Poecile carolinensis

YEAR-ROUND

Size: 5" (13 cm)

Male: Mostly gray with a black cap and chin. White face and chest with a tan belly. Darker-gray tail.

Female: same as male

Juvenile: same as adults

Nest: cavity; female and male build or excavate; 1–2 broods per year

Eggs: 5–7; white with reddish-brown markings

Incubation: 11–12 days; female and male incubate

Fledging: 13–17 days; female and male feed the young

Migration: non-migrator

Food: insects, seeds, fruit; comes to seed and suet feeders

Compare: The Black-capped Chickadee (p. 209) is identical, except in song. The Tufted Titmouse (p. 219) is a close relative but has an erect crest and lacks the black cap and chin.

Stan's Notes: A common chickadee of southern Ohio, spreading northward in the state. Breeds (hybridizes) with the Black-capped Chickadee where their ranges overlap. One of the first birds to use a newly placed feeder. Flies to a feeder, grabs a seed and carries it to a branch. To get to the meat inside, it holds the seed down with its feet and hammers the shell open with its bill. Returns for another seed. A friendly bird. Can be tamed and hand fed. Attracted with a nest box that has a 1¼-inch entrance hole. Female gives a loud snake-like hiss if disturbed on the nest. Often seen with other birds (mixed flock) in winter. Song is a high, fast "chika-dee-dee-dee-dee."

male

female

White-breasted Nuthatch
Sitta carolinensis

YEAR-ROUND

Size: 5–6" (13–15 cm)

Male: Slate gray with a white face, breast and belly. Large white patch on the rump. Black cap and nape. Bill is long and thin, slightly upturned. Chestnut undertail.

Female: similar to male, but has a gray cap and nape

Juvenile: similar to female

Nest: cavity; female and male build a nest within; 1 brood per year

Eggs: 5–7; white with brown markings

Incubation: 11–12 days; female incubates

Fledging: 13–14 days; female and male feed the young

Migration: non-migrator

Food: insects, insect eggs, seeds; comes to seed and suet feeders

Compare: The Red-breasted Nuthatch (p. 207) is smaller and has a rust-red belly and distinctive black eye line. Look for the white breast to help identify the White-breasted Nuthatch.

Stan's Notes: The nuthatch hops headfirst down trees, looking for insects missed by birds climbing up. Its climbing agility is due to an extra-long hind toe claw, or nail, that is nearly twice the size of its front claws. "Nuthatch," from the Middle English *nuthak*, refers to the bird's habit of wedging a seed in a crevice and hacking it open. Often seen in flocks with chickadees, Brown Creepers and Downy Woodpeckers. Mates stay together year-round, defending a small territory. Gives a characteristic "whi-whi-whi-whi" spring call during February and March.

male

female

first winter

WINTER

Yellow-rumped Warbler
Setophaga coronata

Size: 5–6" (13–15 cm)

Male: Slate gray with black streaking on the chest. Yellow patches on the head, flanks and rump. White chin and belly. 2 white wing bars.

Female: duller gray than the male, mixed with brown

Juvenile: first winter is similar to the adult female

Nest: cup; female builds; 2 broods per year

Eggs: 4–5; white with brown markings

Incubation: 12–13 days; female incubates

Fledging: 10–12 days; female and male feed the young

Migration: complete, to Ohio, southern states, Mexico and Central America

Food: insects, berries; visits suet feeders in spring

Compare: The male Yellow Warbler (p. 301) is yellow with orange streaking on its chest. The Chestnut-sided Warbler (p. 89) has chestnut flanks and lacks the yellow rump. Look for yellow patches to help identify the Yellow-rumped.

Stan's Notes: One of the first warblers to migrate in spring. Seems to prefer deciduous woods and forest edges but may be seen in any habitat during migration. Familiar call is a single robust "chip," heard mostly during migration and winter. Sings a wonderful song in spring. Comes to suet feeders in spring, when insect populations are low. Moves quickly among trees and from the ground to trees. Flits around the upper branches of tall trees. In the fall, the male molts to a dull color similar to the female, but he retains his yellow patches all year. Also called Myrtle Warbler. Sometimes called Butter-butt due to the yellow patch on its rump.

female
p. 109

male

Dark-eyed Junco
Junco hyemalis

YEAR-ROUND WINTER

Size: 5½" (14 cm)

Male: Plump, dark-eyed bird with a slate-gray to charcoal chest, head and back. White belly. Pink bill. White outer tail feathers appear like a white V in flight.

Female: round with brown plumage

Juvenile: similar to female, with streaking on the breast and head

Nest: cup; female and male build; 2 broods per year

Eggs: 3–5; white with reddish-brown markings

Incubation: 12–13 days; female incubates

Fledging: 10–13 days; male and female feed the young

Migration: complete, throughout the U.S.

Food: seeds, insects; visits ground and seed feeders

Compare: Rarely confused with any other bird. Look for the pink bill and small flocks feeding under feeders to identify the male Dark-eyed Junco.

Stan's Notes: One of the most common winter birds in the state. Migrates from Canada to Ohio and to areas farther south. Adheres to a rigid social hierarchy, with dominant birds chasing the less dominant ones. Look for the white outer tail feathers flashing in flight. Often seen in small flocks on the ground, where it uses its feet to simultaneously "double-scratch" to expose seeds and insects. Eats many weed seeds. Nests in a wide variety of wooded habitats. Several subspecies of Dark-eyed Junco were previously considered to be separate species. Males don't go as far south as females in winter.

Tufted Titmouse
Baeolophus bicolor

YEAR-ROUND

Size: 6" (15 cm)

Male: Slate gray with a white chest and belly. Pointed crest. Rust-brown wash on the flanks. Gray legs and dark eyes.

Female: same as male

Juvenile: same as adults

Nest: cavity; female lines an old woodpecker cavity; 2 broods per year

Eggs: 5–7; white with brown markings

Incubation: 13–14 days; female incubates

Fledging: 15–18 days; female and male feed the young

Migration: non-migrator

Food: insects, seeds, fruit; will come to seed and suet feeders

Compare: The Black-capped Chickadee (p. 209) is a close relative but is smaller and lacks a crest. The White-breasted Nuthatch (p. 213) has a rust-brown undertail. Look for the pointed crest to help identify the Tufted Titmouse.

Stan's Notes: A common feeder bird that can be attracted with an offering of black oil sunflower seeds or suet. Can also be attracted with a nest box. Well known for its "peter-peter-peter" call, which it quickly repeats. Notorious for pulling hair from sleeping dogs, cats and squirrels to line its nest. Usually seen only one or two at a time. Male feeds female during courtship and nesting. The prefix *tit* in the common name comes from a Scandinavian word meaning "little." Suffix *mouse* is derived from the Old English word *mase*, meaning "bird." Simply translated, it is a "small bird."

Eastern Phoebe
Sayornis phoebe

SUMMER

Size:	7" (18 cm)
Male:	plain gray with slightly darker wings, a light-olive belly and a thin, dark bill
Female:	same as male
Juvenile:	same as adults
Nest:	cup; female builds; 2 broods per year
Eggs:	4–5; white without markings
Incubation:	15–16 days; female incubates
Fledging:	15–16 days; male and female feed the young
Migration:	complete, to southern states and Mexico
Food:	insects
Compare:	The Gray Catbird (p. 229) has a black crown and a chestnut patch under its tail. The Eastern Phoebe lacks any distinctive markings. Listen for its well-enunciated "fee-bee" call and look for the hawking and tail-pumping behaviors to help identify this bird.

Stan's Notes: A sparrow-size bird that often perches on the end of a dead branch. Found in forests, yards and farms. In a process called hawking, it waits for a passing insect. When a bug flies near, it launches out to catch it and then returns to the same branch. It has a distinctive habit of pumping its tail up and down while perching. Builds nest beneath the eaves of houses, under bridges or in other sheltered spots. Uses mud, grass and moss for nest materials and hair (and sometimes feathers) for the lining. The common name is derived from its distinct "fee-bee" call, which it repeats over and over from the top of dead branches.

Eastern Kingbird
Tyrannus tyrannus

SUMMER

Size:	8" (20 cm)
Male:	Mostly gray and black with a white chin and belly. Black head and tail with a distinct white band on the tip of the tail. Concealed red crown, rarely seen.
Female:	same as male
Juvenile:	same as adults
Nest:	cup; male and female build; 1 brood per year
Eggs:	3–4; white with brown markings
Incubation:	16–18 days; female incubates
Fledging:	16–18 days; female and male feed the young
Migration:	complete, to Mexico, Central America and South America
Food:	insects, fruit
Compare:	The American Robin (p. 231) is larger and has a rust-red breast. The Eastern Phoebe (p. 221) is smaller and has an olive-green belly. Look for the white tail band to identify the Kingbird.

Stan's Notes: A summer resident in open fields and prairies. As many as 20 birds migrate in a group. Returns to the mating ground in spring, where pairs defend their territory. Seems to be unafraid of other birds and chases larger birds. Given the common name "King" for its bold attitude and behavior. In a hunting technique known as hawking, it perches on a branch and watches for insects, flies out to catch one, and then returns to the same perch. Swoops from perch to perch when hunting. Becomes very vocal during late summer, when family members call back and forth to one another while hunting for insects.

Great Crested Flycatcher
Myiarchus crinitus

Size: 8" (20 cm)

Male: Gray head with a prominent crest. Gray back and throat. Yellow from the belly to the base of a reddish-brown tail. Lower bill is yellow at the base.

Female: same as male

Juvenile: same as adults

Nest: cavity; female and male stuff a vacant woodpecker cavity or nest box; 1 brood per year

Eggs: 4–6; white to buff with brown markings

Incubation: 13–15 days; female incubates

Fledging: 14–21 days; female and male feed the young

Migration: complete, to Mexico and Central America

Food: insects, fruit

Compare: The Eastern Kingbird (p. 223) has a white band across its tail. The Eastern Phoebe (p. 221) is similar, but it lacks a crest and yellow belly. Look for the crest to identify the Flycatcher.

Stan's Notes: A common bird of wooded areas throughout the state. It lives high up in trees, rarely coming to the ground. Makes long flights from treetop to treetop, moving from one hunting area to another. Gleans insects from tree leaves. Often heard before seen. "Great Crested" refers to the set of extra-long feathers on top of its head (crest), which the bird raises when alert or agitated, like the Northern Cardinal. Nests in an old woodpecker hole but can be attracted with a man-made nest box that has an entrance hole 1½–2½ inches (4–6 cm) in diameter. Often stuffs the cavity with a collection of fur, feathers, string and snake skins.

red morph

gray morph

Eastern Screech-Owl
Megacops asio

YEAR-ROUND

Size: 8–10" (20–25 cm); up to 2' wingspan

Male: Small "eared" owl that occurs in different colorations. Gray morph is mottled gray and white. Red morph is mottled rust and white. Short wings. Bright-yellow eyes.

Female: same as male but slightly larger

Juvenile: lighter color than adults of the same morph and usually lacks ear tufts

Nest: cavity, old woodpecker cavity or man-made nest box; does not add any nesting material; 1 brood per year

Eggs: 4–5; white without markings

Incubation: 25–26 days; female incubates, male feeds the female during incubation

Fledging: 26–27 days; male and female feed the young

Migration: non-migrator; moves around in winter

Food: large insects, small mammals, birds, snakes

Compare: This is the only small owl in Ohio with ear tufts. Can be gray or rust in color.

Stan's Notes: Commonly found in forests that have suitable natural cavities for nesting and roosting. Active from dusk to dawn. Usually gives a tremulous, descending trill, like a sound effect in a scary movie. Seldom gives a screeching call. Often seen sunning itself at a nest-box hole during winter. Mates may have a long-term pair bond and may roost together at night. Excellent hearing and eyesight. Flaps rapidly and flies silently. Has winter and summer territories. The gray morph is more common than the red.

Gray Catbird
Dumetella carolinensis

SUMMER

Size: 9" (23 cm)

Male: Handsome slate-gray bird with a black crown and a long, thin, black bill. Often lifts up its tail, exposing a chestnut patch beneath.

Female: same as male

Juvenile: same as adults

Nest: cup; female and male build; 2 broods per year

Eggs: 4–6; blue green without markings

Incubation: 12–13 days; female incubates

Fledging: 10–11 days; female and male feed the young

Migration: complete, to southern states

Food: insects, occasional fruit; visits suet feeders

Compare: The Eastern Phoebe (p. 221) is smaller and has an olive belly. The Eastern Kingbird (p. 223) is similar in size but has a white belly and a white band across its tail. To identify the Gray Catbird, look for the black crown and chestnut patch under the tail.

Stan's Notes: A secretive bird, more often heard than seen. The Chippewa Indians gave it a name that means "the bird that cries with grief" due to its raspy call. Called "Catbird" because the sound is like the meowing of a house cat. Often mimics other birds, rarely repeating the same phrases. Found in forest edges, backyards and parks. Builds its nest with small twigs. Nests in thick shrubs and quickly flies back into shrubs if approached. If a cowbird lays an egg in its nest, the catbird will quickly break it and eject it.

American Robin
Turdus migratorius

YEAR-ROUND

Size: 9–11" (23–28 cm)

Male: Familiar gray bird with a dark rust-red breast and a nearly black head and tail. White chin with black streaks. White eye-ring.

Female: similar to male, with a duller rust-red breast and a gray head

Juvenile: similar to female, with a speckled breast and brown back

Nest: cup; female builds with help from the male; 2–3 broods per year

Eggs: 4–7; pale blue without markings

Incubation: 12–14 days; female incubates

Fledging: 14–16 days; female and male feed the young

Migration: non-migrator to partial in Ohio

Food: insects, fruit, berries, earthworms

Compare: Familiar bird to all. To differentiate the male from the female, compare the nearly black head and rust-red chest of the male with the gray head and duller chest of the female.

Stan's Notes: Can be heard singing all night in spring. City robins sing louder than country robins in order to hear one another over traffic and noise. A robin isn't listening for worms when it turns its head to one side. It is focusing its sight out of one eye to look for dirt moving, which is caused by worms moving. Territorial, often fighting its reflection in a window. Males have dark heads and a brighter red breast than females. In winter, it switches its diet from insects to fruit.

displaying

Northern Mockingbird
Mimus polyglottos

YEAR-ROUND
SUMMER
MIGRATION

Size: 10" (25 cm)

Male: Silvery-gray head and back with a light-gray breast and belly. White wing patches, seen in flight or during display. Tail mostly black with white outer tail feathers. Black bill.

Female: same as male

Juvenile: dull gray with a heavily streaked breast and a gray bill

Nest: cup; female and male construct; 2 broods per year, sometimes more

Eggs: 3–5; blue green with brown markings

Incubation: 12–13 days; female incubates

Fledging: 11–13 days; female and male feed the young

Migration: non-migrator to partial in Ohio; moves around to find food

Food: insects, fruit

Compare: The Gray Catbird (p. 229) is slate gray and lacks wing patches. Look for the Mockingbird to spread its wings, flash its white wing patches and wag its tail from side to side.

Stan's Notes: A very animated bird. Performs an elaborate mating dance. Facing each other with heads and tails erect, pairs will run toward each other, flashing their white wing patches, and then retreat to cover nearby. Thought to flash the wing patches to scare up insects when hunting. Sits for long periods on top of shrubs. Imitates other birds (vocal mimicry); hence the common name. Young males often sing at night. Often unafraid of people, allowing for close observation.

soaring

juvenile

Sharp-shinned Hawk
Accipiter striatus

YEAR-ROUND
WINTER

Size: 10–14" (25–36 cm); up to 2' wingspan

Male: Small woodland hawk with a gray back and head and a rust-red chest. Short wings. Long, squared tail and several dark tail bands, with the widest at the end of the tail. Red eyes.

Female: same as male but larger

Juvenile: same size as adults, with a brown back, heavy streaking on the chest and yellow eyes

Nest: platform; female builds; 1 brood per year

Eggs: 4–5; white with brown markings

Incubation: 32–35 days; female incubates

Fledging: 24–27 days; female and male feed the young

Migration: complete, to Ohio, southern states, Mexico and Central America

Food: birds, small mammals

Compare: Cooper's Hawk (p. 241) is much larger and has a larger head, a slightly longer neck and a rounded tail. Look for the squared tail to help identify the Sharp-shinned Hawk.

Stan's Notes: A common hawk of backyards, parks and woodlands. Constructs its nest with sticks, usually high in a tree. Typically seen swooping in on birds visiting feeders and chasing them as they flee. Its short wingspan and long tail help it to maneuver through thick stands of trees in pursuit of prey. Calls a loud, high-pitched "kik-kik-kik-kik." Named "Sharp-shinned" for the sharp projection (keel) on the leading edge of its shin. A bird's shin is actually below the ankle (rather than above it, like ours) on the tarsus bone of its foot. In most birds, the tarsus bone is rounded, not sharp.

Eurasian Collared-Dove
Streptopelia decaocto

Size: 12½" (32 cm)

Male: Head, neck, breast and belly are gray to tan. Back, wings and tail are slightly darker. Thin black collar with a white border on the nape of the neck. Tail is long and squared.

Female: same as male

Juvenile: similar to adults

Nest: platform; female and male build; 2–3 broods per year

Eggs: 3–5; cream white without markings

Incubation: 12–14 days; female and male incubate

Fledging: 12–14 days; female and male feed the young

Migration: non-migrator

Food: seeds; will visit ground and seed feeders

Compare: The Mourning Dove (p. 157) is slightly smaller and darker. The Rock Pigeon (p. 239) has colorful iridescent patches. Look for the black collar on the nape and the squared tail to help identify the Eurasian Collared-Dove.

Stan's Notes: A non-native bird. Moved into Florida in the 1980s after inadvertent introduction to the Bahamas; reached Ohio and other northern states in the early 2000s. It has been expanding its range across North America and is predicted to spread just like it did through Europe from Asia. Unknown how this "new" bird will affect populations of the native Mourning Dove. Nearly identical to the Ringed Turtle-Dove, a common pet bird. The dark mark on the back of the neck gave rise to the common name. Look for flashes of white in the tail and dark wing tips when it lands or takes off.

Rock Pigeon
Columba livia

Size: 13" (33 cm)

Male: No set color pattern. Shades of gray to white with patches of gleaming, iridescent green and blue. Often has a light rump patch.

YEAR-ROUND

Female: same as male

Juvenile: same as adults

Nest: platform; female builds; 3–4 broods per year

Eggs: 1–2; white without markings

Incubation: 18–20 days; female and male incubate

Fledging: 25–26 days; female and male feed the young

Migration: non-migrator

Food: seeds, fruit; visits ground and seed feeders

Compare: The Eurasian Collared-Dove (p. 237) has a black collar on the nape. The Mourning Dove (p. 157) is smaller and light brown and lacks the variety of color combinations of the Rock Pigeon.

Stan's Notes: Also known as the Domestic Pigeon. Formerly known as the Rock Dove. Introduced to North America from Europe by the early settlers. Most common around cities and barnyards, where it scratches for seeds. One of the few birds with a wide variety of colors, produced by years of selective breeding while in captivity. Parents feed the young a regurgitated liquid known as crop-milk for the first few days of life. One of the few birds that can drink without tilting its head back. Nests under bridges or on buildings, balconies, barns and sheds. Was once thought to be a nuisance in cities and was poisoned. Now, many cities have Peregrine Falcons feeding on Rock Pigeons, which keeps their numbers in check.

soaring

juvenile

Cooper's Hawk
Accipiter cooperii

YEAR-ROUND

Size: 14–20" (36–51 cm); up to 3' wingspan

Male: Medium-size hawk with short wings and a long, rounded tail with several black bands. Slate-gray back, rusty breast, dark wing tips. Gray bill with a bright-yellow spot at the base. Dark-red eyes.

Female: similar to male but larger

Juvenile: brown back, brown streaking on the breast, bright-yellow eyes

Nest: platform; male and female construct; 1 brood per year

Eggs: 2–4; greenish with brown markings

Incubation: 32–36 days; female and male incubate

Fledging: 28–32 days; male and female feed the young

Migration: non-migrator to partial, to Ohio, southern states and Mexico; moves around to find food

Food: small birds, mammals

Compare: The Sharp-shinned Hawk (p. 235) is much smaller and lighter gray and has a squared tail. Look for the banded, rounded tail to help identify Cooper's Hawk.

Stan's Notes: Found in many habitats, from woodlands to parks and backyards. Stubby wings help it to navigate around trees while it chases small birds. Will ambush prey, flying into heavy brush or even running on the ground in pursuit. Comes to feeders, hunting for birds. Flies with long glides followed by a few quick flaps. Calls a loud, clear "cack-cack-cack-cack." The young have gray eyes that turn bright yellow at 1 year and turn dark red later, after 3–5 years.

juvenile

in-flight
juvenile

in flight

Peregrine Falcon
Falco peregrinus

YEAR-ROUND

Size:	16–20" (41–51 cm); up to 3¾' wingspan
Male:	Dark-gray back, dark "hood" head marking, wide black mustache and tan to white chest. Horizontal bars on belly, legs and undertail. Yellow base of bill, eye-ring and legs.
Female:	similar to male but noticeably larger
Juvenile:	overall darker than adults, with heavy streaking on the chest and belly
Nest:	ground (scrape) on a cliff edge, tall building, bridge or smokestack; 1 brood per year
Eggs:	3–4; white, some with brown markings
Incubation:	29–32 days; female and male incubate
Fledging:	35–42 days; male and female feed the young
Migration:	complete to non-migrator, to southern states
Food:	birds (Rock Pigeons in cities, shorebirds and waterfowl in rural areas)
Compare:	The American Kestrel (p. 145) is smaller and has 2 vertical black stripes on its face. Look for the dark "hood" head marking and mustache marks to identify the Peregrine Falcon.

Stan's Notes: A wide-bodied raptor that hunts many bird species. The larger females hunt larger prey. Lives in many cities, diving (stooping) on pigeons at speeds of up to 200 mph (322 kph), which knocks them to the ground. Soars with its wings flat, often riding thermals. During courtship, the male brings food to the female and performs aerial displays. Likes to nest on a high ledge or platform for a good view of its territory. A solitary nester and monogamous.

female
p. 183

male

soaring

Northern Harrier
Circus hudsonius

YEAR-ROUND

Size: 18–22" (45–56 cm); up to 4' wingspan

Male: Slender, low-flying hawk. Silver gray with a large white rump patch and white belly. Long tail with faint narrow bands. Black wing tips. Yellow eyes.

Female: dark brown back, brown streaking on breast and belly, large white rump patch, thin black tail bands, black wing tips, yellow eyes

Juvenile: similar to female, with an orange chest

Nest: ground; female and male construct; 1 brood per year

Eggs: 4–8; bluish white without markings

Incubation: 31–32 days; female incubates

Fledging: 30–35 days; male and female feed the young

Migration: non-migrator to partial in Ohio; moves around to find food

Food: mice, snakes, insects, small birds

Compare: Cooper's Hawk (p. 241) has a rusty breast. Look for a low-gliding hawk with a large white rump patch to identify the male Harrier.

Stan's Notes: One of the easiest of hawks to identify. Glides just above theground, following the contours of the land while searching for prey. Holds its wings just above horizontal, tilting back and forth in the wind, similar to Turkey Vultures. Formerly called the Marsh Hawk due to its habit of hunting over marshes. Feeds and nests on the ground. Will also preen and rest on the ground. Unlike other hawks, mainly uses its hearing to find prey, followed by sight. At any age, has a distinctive owl-like face disk.

in flight

Canada Goose
Branta canadensis

YEAR-ROUND

Size:	25–43" (64–109 cm); up to 5½' wingspan
Male:	Large gray goose with a black neck and head. White chin and cheek strap.
Female:	same as male
Juvenile:	same as adults
Nest:	platform on the ground; female constructs; 1 brood per year
Eggs:	5–10; white without markings
Incubation:	25–30 days; female incubates
Fledging:	42–55 days; male and female teach the young to feed
Migration:	non-migrator to partial, to southern states; will move to places with open water
Food:	aquatic plants, insects, seeds
Compare:	rarely confused with any other bird

Stan's Notes: Calls a classic "honk-honk-honk," especially in flight. Flocks fly in a large V when traveling long distances. Begins breeding in the third year. Adults mate for many years. If threatened, they will hiss as a warning. Males stand as sentinels at the edge of their group and will bob their heads and become aggressive if approached. Adults molt their primary flight feathers while raising their young, rendering family groups temporarily flightless. Several subspecies occur in the U.S. Generally eastern groups are paler than western. Their size also varies, decreasing northward. The smallest subspecies is in the Arctic.

in flight

Great Blue Heron
Ardea herodias

YEAR-ROUND

Size: 42–48" (107–122 cm); up to 6' wingspan

Male: Tall and gray. Black eyebrows end in long plumes at the back of the head. Long yellow bill. Long feathers at the base of the neck drop down in a kind of necklace. Long legs.

Female: same as male

Juvenile: same as adults, but more brown than gray, with a black crown; lacks plumes

Nest: platform in a colony; male and female build; 1 brood per year

Eggs: 3–5; blue green without markings

Incubation: 27–28 days; female and male incubate

Fledging: 56–60 days; male and female feed the young

Migration: many migrate; some remain and move around to find open water

Food: small fish, frogs, insects, snakes, baby birds

Compare: The Green Heron (p. 257) is much smaller and has a short neck. The Sandhill Crane (p. 251) has a red cap. Look for the long, yellow bill to help identify the Great Blue Heron.

Stan's Notes: One of the most common herons in Ohio. Found in open water, from small ponds to large lakes. Stalks small fish in shallow water. Will strike at mice, squirrels and nearly anything it comes across. Red-winged Blackbirds will attack it to stop it from taking their babies out of the nest. In flight, it holds its neck in an S shape and slightly cups its wings, while the legs trail straight out behind. Nests in a colony of up to 100 birds. Nests in trees near or hanging over water. Barks like a dog when startled.

in flight

rusty
stain

in-flight
rusty stain

Sandhill Crane
Grus canadensis

SUMMER MIGRATION

Size: 42–48" (107–122 cm); up to 7' wingspan

Male: Elegant gray crane with long legs and neck. Wings and body often rust brown from mud staining. Scarlet-red cap. Yellow to red eyes.

Female: same as male

Juvenile: dull brown with yellow eyes; lacks a red cap

Nest: ground; female and male construct; 1 brood per year

Eggs: 2; olive with brown markings

Incubation: 28–32 days; female and male incubate

Fledging: 65 days; female and male feed the young

Migration: complete, to southern states and Mexico

Food: insects, fruit, worms, plants, amphibians

Compare: The Great Blue Heron (p. 249) has a longer bill and holds its neck in an S shape during flight. Look for the scarlet-red cap to help identify the Sandhill Crane.

Stan's Notes: One of the tallest birds in Ohio. Preens mud into its feathers, staining its plumage rust brown (see insets). Gives a very loud and distinctive rattling call, often heard before the bird is seen. Flight is characteristic, with a faster upstroke, making the wings look like they're flicking in flight. Can fly at heights of over 10,000 feet (3,050 m). Found in wetlands and often seen in large, undisturbed fields close to water. Nests on the ground in a large mound of aquatic vegetation. Performs a spectacular mating dance: The birds will face each other, then bow and jump into the air while making loud cackling sounds and flapping their wings. They will also flip sticks and grass into the air during their dance.

251

male

female

Ruby-throated Hummingbird
Archilochus colubris

SUMMER

Size: 3–3½" (7.5–9 cm)

Male: Tiny, iridescent green bird. Black throat patch reflects bright ruby red in direct sunlight.

Female: same as male but lacks a throat patch

Juvenile: same as female

Nest: cup; female builds; 1–2 broods per year

Eggs: 2; white without markings

Incubation: 12–14 days; female incubates

Fledging: 14–18 days; female feeds the young

Migration: complete, to southern states, Mexico and Central America

Food: nectar, insects; will come to nectar feeders

Compare: No other bird is as tiny. The Sphinx Moth also hovers at flowers but has clear wings, doesn't hum in flight, moves much slower than the Ruby-throated and can be approached.

Stan's Notes: This is the smallest bird in the state. Can fly straight up, straight down or backward and hover in midair. Does not sing but chatters or buzzes to communicate. Weighs about the same as a U.S. penny; it takes about five average-size hummingbirds to equal the weight of one chickadee. The wings create the humming sound. Flaps 50–60 times or more per second when flying at top speed. Breathes 250 times per minute. Heart beats up to 1,260 times per minute. Builds a stretchy nest with plant material and spiderwebs, gluing pieces of lichen to the exterior for camouflage. Attracted to colorful, tubular flowers. Will extract and eat insects trapped in spiderwebs. A long-distance migrator, wintering in the tropics of Central America.

female
p. 179

male

Wood Duck
Aix sponsa

SUMMER

Size:	17–20" (43–51 cm)
Male:	small, highly ornamented dabbling duck with a mostly green head and crest patterned with black and white, a rusty chest, a white belly and red eyes
Female:	brown duck with a bright-white eye-ring, not-so-obvious crest and blue patch on wings (speculum), often hidden
Juvenile:	similar to female
Nest:	cavity; female lines an old woodpecker cavity or a nest box in a tree; 1 brood per year
Eggs:	10–15; cream white without markings
Incubation:	28–36 days; female incubates
Fledging:	56–68 days; female teaches the young to feed
Migration:	complete, to southern states
Food:	aquatic insects, plants, seeds
Compare:	More colorful than the male Green-winged Teal (p. 163). Lacks the large, wide bill of the male Northern Shoveler (p. 261).

Stan's Notes: A common duck of quiet, shallow backwater ponds. Nearly went extinct around 1900 due to overhunting, but it's doing well now. Nests in a tree cavity or a nest box in a tree. Seen flying in forests or perching on high branches. Female takes off with a loud squealing call and enters the nest cavity from full flight. Lays some eggs in a neighboring nest (egg dumping), resulting in more than 20 eggs in some clutches. Hatchlings stay in the nest for 24 hours, then jump from as high as 60 feet (18 m) to the ground or water to follow their mother. They never return to the nest.

Green Heron
Butorides virescens

SUMMER

Size: 16–22" (41–56 cm)

Male: Short and stocky. Blue-green back and rust-red neck and breast. Dark-green crest. Short legs are normally yellow but turn bright orange during the breeding season.

Female: same as male

Juvenile: similar to adults, with a bluish-gray back and white-streaked breast and neck

Nest: platform; female and male build; 2 broods per year

Eggs: 2–4; light green without markings

Incubation: 21–25 days; female and male incubate

Fledging: 35–36 days; female and male feed the young

Migration: complete, to southern states, Mexico, and Central and South America

Food: small fish, aquatic insects, small amphibians

Compare: The Great Blue Heron (p. 249) is larger and has long legs. Look for a small heron with a green back and crest to identify the Green.

Stan's Notes: Often gives an explosive, rasping "skyew" call when startled. Holds its head close to its body, which sometimes makes it look like it doesn't have a neck. Makes short, quick flights across the water. Waits on the shore or wades stealthily, hunting for small fish, aquatic insects and small amphibians. Places an object, such as an insect, on the water's surface to attract fish to catch. Raises its crest when excited. Nests in a tall tree, often a short distance from the water. The nest can be very high up in the tree. Babies give a loud ticking sound, like the ticktock of a clock.

female
p. 189

male

Mallard

Anas platyrhynchos

YEAR-ROUND

Size: 19–21" (48–53 cm)

Male: Large, bulbous green head, white necklace and rust-brown or chestnut chest. Gray-and-white sides. Yellow bill. Orange legs and feet.

Female: brown with an orange-and-black bill and blue-and-white wing mark (speculum)

Juvenile: same as female but with a yellow bill

Nest: ground; female builds; 1 brood per year

Eggs: 7–10; greenish to whitish, unmarked

Incubation: 26–30 days; female incubates

Fledging: 42–52 days; female leads the young to food

Migration: non-migrator in Ohio; moves around to find food

Food: seeds, plants, aquatic insects; will come to ground feeders offering corn

Compare: Most people recognize this common duck. The male Northern Shoveler (p. 261) has a white chest with rusty sides and a very large, spoon-shaped bill. Look for the green head and yellow bill to identify the male Mallard.

Stan's Notes: A familiar dabbling duck of lakes and ponds. Also found in rivers, streams and some backyards. Tips forward to feed on vegetation on the bottom of shallow water. The name "Mallard" comes from the Latin word *masculus,* meaning "male," referring to the male's habit of taking no part in raising the young. Male and female have white underwings and white tails, but only the male has black central tail feathers that curl upward. Unlike the female, the male doesn't quack. Returns to its birthplace each year.

female
p. 191

male

Northern Shoveler
Spatula clypeata

Size: 19–21" (48–53 cm)

Male: Medium-size duck with an iridescent green head, rust sides, white chest. Extraordinarily large, spoon-shaped bill, almost always held pointed toward the water.

Female: brown and black, with a green wing patch (speculum) and large, spoon-shaped bill

Juvenile: same as female

Nest: ground; female builds; 1 brood per year

Eggs: 9–12; olive without markings

Incubation: 22–25 days; female incubates

Fledging: 30–60 days; female leads the young to food

Migration: complete, to southern states, Mexico and Central America

Food: aquatic insects, plants

Compare: The male Mallard (p. 259) is similar but lacks the large, spoon-shaped bill. The male Wood Duck (p. 255) is smaller and has a crest.

Stan's Notes: One of several species of shovelers. Called "Shoveler" due to the peculiar, shovel-like shape of its bill. Given the common name "Northern" because it is the only species of these ducks in North America. Seen in shallow wetlands, ponds and small lakes in flocks of 5–10 birds. Flocks fly in tight formation. Swims low in water, pointing its large bill toward the water as if it's too heavy to lift. Usually swims in tight circles while feeding. Feeds mainly by filtering tiny aquatic insects and plants from the surface of the water with its bill. Female gathers plant material and forms it into a nest a short distance from the water.

in flight

female
p. 281

male

Common Merganser
Mergus merganser

MIGRATION

Size: 26–28" (66–71 cm)

Male: Long, thin, duck-like bird with a green head and black back. White sides, chest and neck. Long, pointed, orange bill. Often looks black and white in poor light.

Female: Same size and shape as the male, with a rust-red head and ragged "hair," gray body, white chest and chin.

Juvenile: same as female

Nest: cavity; female lines an old woodpecker hole or a natural cavity; 1 brood per year

Eggs: 9–11; ivory without markings

Incubation: 28–33 days; female incubates

Fledging: 70–80 days; female feeds the young

Migration: complete, to southern states, Mexico and Central America

Food: small fish, aquatic insects, amphibians

Compare: The male Mallard (p. 259) is smaller and lacks the black back and long, pointed, orange bill.

Stan's Notes: Seen on any open water during the winter but more common along large rivers than lakes. A large, shallow-water diver that feeds on fish in 10–15 feet (3–4.5 m) of water. Bill has a fine, serrated-like edge that helps catch slippery fish. Female often lays some eggs in other merganser nests (egg dumping), resulting in up to 15 young in some broods. Male leaves female once she starts incubating. Orphans are accepted by other merganser mothers with young. Fast flight, often low and close to the water, in groups but not in formation. Usually not vocal except for an alarm call.

female
p. 297

male

American Redstart

Setophaga ruticilla

SUMMER MIGRATION

Size:	5" (13 cm)
Male:	striking black warbler with orange patches on the sides, wings and tail; white belly
Female:	olive brown with yellow patches on the sides, wings and tail, white belly
Juvenile:	same as female; male attains orange tinges in the second year
Nest:	cup; female builds; 1 brood per year
Eggs:	3–5; off-white with brown markings
Incubation:	12 days; female incubates
Fledging:	9 days; female and male feed the young
Migration:	complete, to Mexico, Central America and South America
Food:	insects, seeds, occasionally berries
Compare:	The male Baltimore Oriole (p. 267) and male Red-winged Blackbird (p. 29) are much larger. The male American Redstart is the only small black-and-orange bird flitting around the top of trees.

Stan's Notes: One of the most common and widespread warblers in Ohio. Found in woodlands, parks and yards and at forest edges. Prefers large, unbroken tracts of forest. Appears hyperactive when it feeds, hovering and darting back and forth to glean insects from leaves. Often droops wings and fans tail before launching out to catch an insect. Look for the flashing black-and-orange colors of the male high up in trees. First-year males have yellow markings and look like the females. Sings a high-pitched song that builds in intensity and then suddenly ends.

female
p. 307

male

Baltimore Oriole
Icterus galbula

SUMMER

Size: 7–8" (18–20 cm)

Male: Flaming orange with a black head and back. White-and-orange wing bars. Orange-and-black tail. Gray bill and dark eyes.

Female: pale yellow with orange tones, gray-brown wings, white wing bars, gray bill, dark eyes

Juvenile: same as female

Nest: pendulous; female builds; 1 brood per year

Eggs: 4–5; bluish with brown markings

Incubation: 12–14 days; female incubates

Fledging: 12–14 days; female and male feed the young

Migration: complete, to Mexico, Central America and South America

Food: insects, fruit, nectar; comes to nectar, orange-half and grape-jelly feeders

Compare: The male American Redstart (p. 265) has much less orange. The male Orchard Oriole (p. 269) is much darker orange. Look for the flaming orange to identify the male Baltimore Oriole.

Stan's Notes: A fantastic songster, often heard before seen. Easily attracted to a feeder that offers sugar water (nectar), orange halves or grape jelly. Parents bring their young to feeders. Sits at the top of trees, feeding on caterpillars. Female builds a sock-like nest at the outermost branches of tall trees. Prefers parks, yards and forests and often returns to the same area year after year. Seen during migration and summer. Some of the last birds to arrive in spring (May) and some of the first to leave in the fall (September). Young males turn orange-and-black at 1½ years of age.

female
p. 309

male

first-year
male

Orchard Oriole
Icterus spurius

SUMMER MIGRATION

Size: 7–8" (18–20 cm)

Male: Dark-orange with black head, throat, upper back, wings and tail. White wing bar. Bill is long and thin. Gray mark on lower bill.

Female: olive-green back, dull-yellow belly and gray wings with 2 indistinct white wing bars

Juvenile: same as female; first-year male looks like the female, with a black bib

Nest: pendulous; female builds; 1 brood per year

Eggs: 3–5; pale blue to white, brown markings

Incubation: 11–12 days; female and male incubate

Fledging: 11–14 days; female and male feed the young

Migration: complete, to Mexico, Central America and northern South America

Food: insects, fruit, nectar; comes to nectar, orange-half and grape-jelly feeders

Compare: The male Baltimore Oriole (p. 267) is brighter orange. The male American Redstart (p. 265) has a white belly. Look for the dark orange plumage to identify the male Orchard Oriole.

Stan's Notes: Named "Orchard" for its preference for orchards. Also likes open woods. Eats insects until wild fruit starts to ripen. Often nests alone; sometimes nests in small colonies. Parents bring their young to bird feeding stations after they fledge. Many people don't see these birds at their feeders very much during the summer and think they have left, but the birds are still there, hunting for insects to feed to their young. Some of the first birds to migrate at the end of summer. Often migrates in flocks with Baltimore Orioles.

male

female
p. 101

yellow
male

House Finch
Haemorhous mexicanus

YEAR-ROUND

Size: 5" (13 cm)

Male: Small finch with a red to orange face, throat, chest and rump. Brown cap. Brown marking behind eyes. White belly with brown streaks. Brown wings with white streaks.

Female: brown with a heavily streaked white chest

Juvenile: similar to female

Nest: cup, occasionally in a cavity; female builds; 2 broods per year

Eggs: 4–5; pale blue, lightly marked

Incubation: 12–14 days; female incubates

Fledging: 15–19 days; female and male feed the young

Migration: non-migrator to partial; will move around to find food

Food: seeds, fruit, leaf buds; visits seed feeders and feeders that offer grape jelly

Compare: The male Purple Finch (p. 273) has a red cap. Look for the brown cap and streaked belly to help identify the male House Finch.

Stan's Notes: Can be a common bird at your feeders. Very social, visiting feeders in small flocks. Likes to nest in hanging flower baskets. Male sings a loud, cheerful warbling song. It was originally introduced to Long Island, New York, from the western U.S. in the 1940s and is now found throughout the country. Suffers from a disease that causes the eyes to crust, resulting in blindness and death. Rarely, males are yellow (inset), perhaps due to poor diet.

female
p. 117

male

Purple Finch
Haemorhous purpureus

Size: 6" (15 cm)

Male: Raspberry-red head, cap, chest, back and rump. Brownish wings and tail. Large bill.

YEAR-ROUND WINTER

Female: heavily streaked brown-and-white bird with bold white eyebrows

Juvenile: same as female

Nest: cup; female and male build; 1 brood per year

Eggs: 4–5; greenish blue with brown markings

Incubation: 12–13 days; female incubates

Fledging: 13–14 days; female and male feed the young

Migration: irruptive; moves around in winter to find food

Food: seeds, insects, fruit; comes to seed feeders

Compare: The male House Finch (p. 271) has a brown cap and a streaked belly. Look for the raspberry cap to help identify the male Purple Finch.

Stan's Notes: A year-round resident of northeastern Ohio. More commonly seen during migration in the rest of the state. Long-term residency in Ohio, unlike the recent invasion of the House Finch. Travels in flocks of up to 50 birds. Visits seed feeders along with House Finches, which makes it hard to tell them apart. Feeds mainly on seeds; ash tree seeds are an important source of food. Found in coniferous forests, mixed woods, woodland edges and suburban backyards. Flies in the typical undulating, up-and-down pattern of finches. Sings a rich, loud song. Gives a distinctive "tic" note only in flight. Male is not purple. The Latin species name *purpureus* means "purple" (or other reddish colors).

female
p. 305

male

Scarlet Tanager
Piranga olivacea

SUMMER

Size:	7" (18 cm)
Male:	Bright scarlet with coal-black wings and tail. Ivory bill and dark eyes.
Female:	drab greenish yellow with olive wings and tail, whitish wing linings and dark eyes
Juvenile:	same as female
Nest:	cup; female builds; 1 brood per year
Eggs:	4–5; blue green with brown markings
Incubation:	13–14 days; female incubates
Fledging:	9–11 days; female and male feed the young
Migration:	complete, to Central and South America
Food:	insects, fruit
Compare:	The male Northern Cardinal (p. 277) is larger, with a black mask and red bill. Look for the black wings and tail to help identify the male Scarlet Tanager.

Stan's Notes: A tropical-looking bird. Found in mature deciduous woodlands, where it hunts for insects high up in trees. Requires a territory covering at least 4 acres (1.5 ha) for nesting but prefers 8 acres (3 ha). Arrives late in spring and leaves early in fall. Male and female both sing like American Robins, but the tanagers intersperse an unusual "chick-burr" call in their songs. The song of the female is like that of the male, only softer. This bird is one of hundreds of tanager species in the world. Nearly all are brightly colored and live in the tropics. The name "Tanager" comes from a South American Tupi Indian word meaning "any small, brightly colored bird." The male sheds (molts) his bright-scarlet plumage in the fall, appearing more like the female during winter.

female
p. 137

male

juvenile

Northern Cardinal
Cardinalis cardinalis

YEAR-ROUND

Size: 8–9" (20–23 cm)

Male: Red with a black mask that extends from the face to the throat. Large crest and a large red bill.

Female: buff brown with a black mask, large reddish bill, and red tinges on the crest and wings

Juvenile: same as female but with a blackish-gray bill

Nest: cup; female builds; 2–3 broods per year

Eggs: 3–4; bluish white with brown markings

Incubation: 12–13 days; female and male incubate

Fledging: 9–10 days; female and male feed the young

Migration: non-migrator

Food: seeds, insects, fruit; comes to seed feeders

Compare: The male Scarlet Tanager (p. 275) is smaller and has black wings. Look for the black mask, large crest and red bill to identify the male Northern Cardinal.

Stan's Notes: A familiar backyard bird. Seen in a variety of habitats, including parks. Usually likes thick vegetation. One of the few species in which both males and females sing. Can be heard all year. Listen for its "whata-cheer-cheer-cheer" territorial call in spring. Watch for a male feeding a female during courtship. The male also feeds the young of the first brood while the female builds a second nest. Territorial in spring, fighting its own reflection in a window or other reflective surface. Non-territorial in winter, gathering in small flocks of up to 20 birds. Makes short flights from cover to cover, often landing on the ground. *Cardinalis* denotes importance, as represented by the red priestly garments of Catholic cardinals.

female p. 187

male

Redhead
Aythya americana

MIGRATION
WINTER

Size: 19" (48 cm)

Male: Rich-red head and neck with a black breast and tail, gray sides, and smoky-gray wings and back. Tricolored bill with a light-blue base, white ring and black tip.

Female: soft-brown, plain-looking duck with gray to white wing linings, a rounded top of head and a gray bill with a black tip

Juvenile: similar to female

Nest: cup; female builds; 1 brood per year

Eggs: 9–14; white without markings

Incubation: 24–28 days; female and male incubate

Fledging: 56–73 days; female shows young what to eat

Migration: complete, to northern Ohio and southern states; moves around to find open water and food

Food: seeds, aquatic plants, insects

Compare: The male Northern Shoveler (p. 261) has a green head and rusty sides, unlike the red head and gray sides of the male Redhead.

Stan's Notes: A duck of permanent large bodies of water. Forages along the shoreline, feeding on seeds, aquatic plants and insects. Usually builds nest directly on the water's surface, using large mats of vegetation. Female lays up to 75 percent of its eggs in the nests of other Redheads and several other duck species. Overall populations seem to be increasing at about 2–3 percent each year.

in flight

male
p. 263

female

Common Merganser

Mergus merganser

MIGRATION

Size: 26–28" (66–71 cm)

Female: Long, thin, duck-like bird with a rust-red head and ragged "hair." Gray body and white chest and chin. Long, pointed, orange bill.

Male: same size and shape as the female, but with a green head, a black back and white sides

Juvenile: same as female

Nest: cavity; female lines an old woodpecker hole or a natural cavity; 1 brood per year

Eggs: 9–11; ivory without markings

Incubation: 28–33 days; female incubates

Fledging: 70–80 days; female feeds the young

Migration: complete, to southern states, Mexico and Central America

Food: small fish, aquatic insects

Compare: Hard to confuse with other birds. Look for a rust-red head with ragged "hair," a white chin and a long, pointed, orange bill to identify.

Stan's Notes: Seen on any open water during the winter but more common along large rivers than lakes. A large, shallow-water diver that feeds on fish in 10–15 feet (3–4.5 m) of water. Bill has a fine, serrated-like edge that helps catch slippery fish. The female often lays some eggs in other merganser nests (egg dumping), resulting in up to 15 young in some broods. Male leaves the female once she starts incubating. Orphans are accepted by other merganser mothers with young. Fast flight, often low and close to the water, in groups but not in formation. Usually not vocal except for an alarm call that sounds like a muffled quack.

in flight

breeding

juvenile

winter

Ring-billed Gull
Larus delawarensis

Size: 18–20" (45–51 cm); up to 4' wingspan

Male: White with gray wings, black wing tips spotted with white, and a white tail, seen in flight (inset). Yellow bill with a black ring near the tip. Yellowish legs and feet. In winter, the back of the head and the nape of the neck are speckled brown.

Female: same as male

Juvenile: white with brown speckles and a brown tip of tail; mostly dark bill

Nest: ground; female and male construct; 1 brood per year

Eggs: 2–4; off-white with brown markings

Incubation: 20–21 days; female and male incubate

Fledging: 20–40 days; female and male feed the young

Migration: complete, to southern states and Mexico; non-migrator along Lake Erie

Food: insects, fish; scavenges for food

Compare: The Herring Gull (p. 285) has an orange-red mark on its lower bill and pinkish legs. Look for the black ring on the bill to help identify the Ring-billed Gull.

Stan's Notes: A common gull of garbage dumps and parking lots. This bird is expanding its range and remaining farther north longer in winter, where it is foraging for food in cities. A three-year gull with different plumages in each of its first three years. Attains the ring on its bill after the first winter and adult plumage in the third year. Defends a small area around the nest, usually only a few feet.

in flight

breeding

juvenile

winter

Herring Gull
Larus argentatus

Size: 23–26" (58–66 cm); up to 5' wingspan

Male: White with slate-gray wings. Black wing tips with tiny white spots. Yellow bill with an orange-red spot near the tip of the lower bill (mandible). Pinkish legs and feet. Winter plumage has gray speckles on head and neck.

Female: same as male

Juvenile: mottled brown to gray, with a black bill

Nest: ground; female and male construct; 1 brood per year

Eggs: 2–3; olive with brown markings

Incubation: 24–28 days; female and male incubate

Fledging: 35–36 days; female and male feed the young

Migration: complete, to southern states; non-migrator along Lake Erie

Food: fish, insects, clams, eggs, baby birds

Compare: Larger than the Ring-billed Gull (p. 283), which has yellowish legs and feet and a black ring on its bill. Look for the orange-red spot on the bill to help identify the Herring Gull.

Stan's Notes: A common gull of large lakes. An opportunistic bird, scavenging for human food in dumpsters, parking lots and other places with garbage. Takes eggs and young from other bird nests. Often drops clams and other shellfish from heights to break the shells and get to the soft interior. Nests in colonies, returning to the same site annually. Lines its nest with grass and seaweed. It takes about four years for the juveniles to obtain adult plumage. Adults have spotted heads during winter.

white
morph

blue morph

juvenile

in flight

Snow Goose
Chen caerulescens

Size: 25–38" (64–97 cm); up to 4½' wingspan

Male: White morph has black wing tips and varying patches of black and brown. Blue morph has a white head and a gray breast and back. Both morphs have a pink bill and legs.

Female: same as male

Juvenile: dull gray with a dark bill

Nest: ground; female builds; 1 brood per year

Eggs: 3–5; white without markings

Incubation: 23–25 days; female incubates

Fledging: 45–49 days; female and male teach the young to feed

Migration: complete, to southern states and Mexico; winters along Lake Erie

Food: aquatic insects and plants

Compare: The Mute Swan (p. 291) is twice the size and lacks the black wing tips of the Snow Goose. The Canada Goose (p. 247) has a black neck and white chin strap.

Stan's Notes: This bird occurs in light (white) and dark (blue) color morphs. The white morph is more common than the blue. A bird of wide-open fields, wetlands and lakes of any size. It has a thick, serrated bill, which helps it to grab and pull up plants. Breeds in large colonies on the northern tundra in Canada. Female starts to breed at 2–3 years. Older females produce more eggs and are more successful at reproduction than younger females. Migrates in huge flocks with thousands of birds. Has a classic goose-like call. When thousands of geese call, it sounds like one constant call.

in flight

Great Egret
Ardea alba

Size: 36–40" (91–102 cm); up to 4½' wingspan

Male: Tall, thin, all-white bird with a long neck and a long, pointed yellow bill. Black, stilt-like legs and black feet.

Female: same as male

Juvenile: same as adults

Nest: platform; male and female construct; 1 brood per year

Eggs: 2–3; light blue without markings

Incubation: 23–26 days; female and male incubate

Fledging: 43–49 days; female and male feed the young

Migration: complete, to southern states, Mexico and Central America

Food: small fish, aquatic insects, frogs, crayfish

Compare: Smaller than the Great Blue Heron (p. 249) but similar in shape. Look for the long, thin white neck and long, pointed, yellow bill to help identify the Great Egret.

Stan's Notes: A graceful, stately bird. Slowly stalks shallow ponds, lakes and wetlands in search of small fish to spear with its long, sharp bill. Holds neck in an S shape during flight. Nests in colonies with as many as 100 birds. Gives a loud, dry croak if disturbed or when squabbling for a nest site at the colony. The name "Egret" comes from the French word *aigrette,* meaning "ornamental tufts of plumes." The plumes grow near the tail during the breeding season. Hunted to near extinction in the 1800s and early 1900s for its beautiful long plumes, which were used to decorate hats for women. Today, the egret is a protected species.

Mute Swan

Cygnus olor

YEAR-ROUND
MIGRATION
WINTER

Size: 60" (152 cm); up to 7' wingspan

Male: White with a large orange bill. Bill has a prominent black knob at the base. Holds its neck in an S shape with bill pointed toward the surface of the water.

Female: same as male

Juvenile: brown to gray with a gray bill with a black base; bill lacks a prominent knob

Nest: ground; female and male construct; 1 brood per year

Eggs: 4–8; light gray without markings

Incubation: 35–40 days; female and male incubate

Fledging: 115–150 days; female and male feed the young

Migration: non-migrator to partial; will move to areas with open water and food during winter

Food: aquatic insects and plants

Compare: hard to confuse with other birds

Stan's Notes: Usually silent, not mute. Makes a variety of sounds, including hisses, barks and snorts, when agitated. An introduced species—frequently to lakes, parks, zoos, golf courses and private property—it is now found in the wild. Often swims with wings arched over its back. Neck is always held in an S shape. Uses neck to reach plants on the bottom of a lake or pond. Forms a long-term pair bond. Pairs defend large territories, driving off any other large birds, including native swans and geese. Some states work to reduce the number of Mute Swans because of the fear of competition with native species.

male

winter
male

female

American Goldfinch
Spinus tristis

YEAR-ROUND

Size: 5" (13 cm)

Male: Canary-yellow finch with a black forehead and tail. Black wings with white wing bars. White rump. No markings on the chest. Winter male is similar to the female.

Female: dull olive-yellow plumage with brown wings; lacks a black forehead

Juvenile: same as female

Nest: cup; female builds; 1 brood per year

Eggs: 4–6; pale blue without markings

Incubation: 10–12 days; female incubates

Fledging: 11–17 days; female and male feed the young

Migration: partial; small flocks of up to 20 birds move around to find food

Food: seeds, insects; comes to seed feeders

Compare: The male Yellow Warbler (p. 301) is yellow with orange streaks on its chest. The Pine Siskin (p. 99) has a streaked chest and belly and yellow wing bars. The female House Finch (p. 101) and female Purple Finch (p. 117) have heavily streaked chests.

Stan's Notes: A common backyard resident. Most often found in open fields, scrubby areas and woodlands. Enjoys Nyjer seed in feeders. Breeds in late summer. Lines its nest with the silky down from wild thistle. Almost always in small flocks. Twitters while it flies. Flight is roller coaster-like. Moves around to find adequate food during winter. Often called Wild Canary due to the male's canary-colored plumage. Male sings a pleasant, high-pitched song.

Common Yellowthroat
Geothlypis trichas

SUMMER

Size: 5" (13 cm)

Male: Olive-brown with a bright-yellow throat and chest, a white belly and a distinctive black mask outlined in white. Long, thin, pointed black bill.

Female: similar to male but lacks a black mask

Juvenile: same as female

Nest: cup; female builds; 2 broods per year

Eggs: 3–5; white with brown markings

Incubation: 11–12 days; female incubates

Fledging: 10–11 days; female and male feed the young

Migration: complete, to southern states, Mexico and Central America

Food: insects

Compare: The male Yellow Warbler (p. 301) has orange streaking on its chest and no mask. The male American Goldfinch (p. 293) has a black forehead and wings. The Yellow-rumped Warbler (p. 215) only has patches of yellow and lacks the yellow chest of the Yellowthroat.

Stan's Notes: A common warbler of open fields and marshes. Sings a cheerful, well-known "witchity-witchity-witchity-witchity" song from deep within tall grasses. Male sings from prominent perches and while he hunts. He performs a curious courtship display, bouncing in and out of tall grass while singing a mating song. Female builds a nest low to the ground. Young remain dependent on their parents longer than most other warblers. A frequent cowbird host.

male
p. 265

female

American Redstart
Setophaga ruticilla

SUMMER MIGRATION

Size: 5" (13 cm)

Female: Olive-brown warbler with yellow patches on the sides, wings and tail. White belly.

Male: black with orange patches on the sides, wings and tail; white belly

Juvenile: same as female; male attains orange tinges in the second year

Nest: cup; female builds; 1 brood per year

Eggs: 3–5; off-white with brown markings

Incubation: 12 days; female incubates

Fledging: 9 days; female and male feed the young

Migration: complete, to Mexico, Central America and South America

Food: insects, seeds, occasionally berries

Compare: The female Yellow-rumped Warbler (p. 215) is similar, but it has a yellow patch on its rump. Look for yellow patches on the sides, wings and tail to help identify the female Redstart.

Stan's Notes: One of the most common and widespread warblers in Ohio. Found in woodlands, parks and yards and at forest edges. Prefers large, unbroken tracts of forest. Appears hyperactive when it feeds, hovering and darting back and forth to glean insects from leaves. Often droops wings and fans tail before launching out to catch an insect. Look for the flashing black-and-orange colors of the male high up in trees. First-year males have yellow markings and look like the females. Sings a high-pitched song that builds in intensity and then suddenly ends.

male

winter male

female

Magnolia Warbler
Setophaga magnolia

SUMMER MIGRATION

Size: 5" (13 cm)

Male: Yellow and black with a gray crown and white eyebrows. Heavy black streaks on a yellow chest and belly. White wing patch. Yellow rump. Obvious white patches on tail.

Female: similar to male but lacks black on the face and has 2 white wing bars

Juvenile: same as female

Nest: cup; female and male build; 1 brood per year

Eggs: 3–5; white with brown markings

Incubation: 11–13 days; female incubates

Fledging: 8–10 days; female and male feed the young

Migration: complete, to Central America

Food: insects

Compare: More yellow than the Yellow-rumped Warbler (p. 215). The Yellow Warbler (p. 301) lacks black on the face and a black back.

Stan's Notes: This warbler is commonly seen during migration. Breeds in only a few select areas in Ohio, nesting in other northern states and Canada. Populations are stable due to the ability to adapt to second-growth forest. Look for it low in trees, where it feeds on insects. Often fans its tail while picking insects from the undersides of leaves. Males often feed higher up in trees than the females. Named "Magnolia" when ornithologist Alexander Wilson saw the species for the first time in a magnolia tree.

male

female

Yellow Warbler
Setophaga petechia

SUMMER

Size: 5" (13 cm)

Male: Yellow with thin orange streaks on the chest and belly. Long, pointed, dark bill.

Female: same as male but lacks orange streaks

Juvenile: similar to female but much duller

Nest: cup; female builds; 1 brood per year

Eggs: 4–5; white with brown markings

Incubation: 11–12 days; female incubates

Fledging: 10–12 days; female and male feed the young

Migration: complete, to southern states, Mexico, and Central and South America

Food: insects

Compare: The Yellow-rumped Warbler (p. 215) has just patches of yellow. The male American Goldfinch (p. 293) has a black forehead and black wings. The female American Goldfinch (p. 293) has white wing bars. Look for the orange streaks on the chest to identify the male Yellow Warbler.

Stan's Notes: Common and widespread. Seen in shrubby areas close to water, gardens and backyards. Zooms around shrubs and shorter trees. A prolific insect eater, gleaning caterpillars and other insects from tree leaves. Male sings loudly, flies off to grab a bug, and then starts singing again. Male sings a string of notes that sound like "sweet, sweet, sweet, I'm-so-sweet!" Begins to migrate south in July and is gone by August. Males arrive in spring before females to claim territories. Migrates at night in mixed flocks of warblers. Rests and feeds during the day.

Palm Warbler
Setophaga palmarum

MIGRATION

Size: 5½" (14 cm)

Male: Distinctive yellow eyebrows. Yellow throat, belly and undertail. Obvious chestnut cap. Thin chestnut streaks on the sides of the breast. Dark line across dark eyes.

Female: same as male

Juvenile: same as adults but duller and brown

Nest: cup; female builds; 1–2 broods per year

Eggs: 4–5; white with brown markings

Incubation: 11–12 days; female incubates

Fledging: 12–13 days; female and male feed the young

Migration: complete, to southeastern states, Caribbean and Central America

Food: insects, fruit

Compare: The Yellow-rumped Warbler (p. 215) is similar in size but lacks the yellow throat and belly of the Palm. The Yellow Warbler (p. 301) is slightly smaller and lacks a chestnut cap. Look for the yellow eyebrows and chestnut cap of the Palm Warbler.

Stan's Notes: One of the most common and abundant warblers. Frequently seen in backyard woodlands during migration. Look for it to wag or bob its tail while gleaning insects from leaves and flowers of trees. One of the few warblers to feed on the ground. Hops rather than walks. Nests at the edges of northern spruce bogs. Recognizes cowbird eggs and destroys them, burying them with its nest, which it builds on top of the cowbird nest.

female

male
p. 275

Scarlet Tanager
Piranga olivacea

SUMMER

Size: 7" (18 cm)

Female: Drab greenish yellow with olive wings and tail. Whitish wing linings. Dark eyes.

Male: bright scarlet with coal-black wings and tail, an ivory bill and dark eyes

Juvenile: same as female

Nest: cup; female builds; 1 brood per year

Eggs: 4–5; blue green with brown markings

Incubation: 13–14 days; female incubates

Fledging: 9–11 days; female and male feed the young

Migration: complete, to Central and South America

Food: insects, fruit

Compare: The female Baltimore Oriole (p. 307) has gray-brown wings. The female American Goldfinch (p. 293) has white wing bars. Look for the olive wings to identify the female Tanager.

Stan's Notes: A tropical-looking bird found in mature deciduous woodlands, where it hunts for insects high up in trees. Requires a territory covering at least 4 acres (1.5 ha) for nesting but prefers 8 acres (3 ha). Arrives late in spring and leaves early in fall. Both the female and male sing like American Robins, but the tanagers intersperse an unusual "chick-burr" call in their songs. The song of the female is like that of the male, only softer. This bird is one of hundreds of tanager species in the world. Nearly all are brightly colored and live in the tropics. The name "Tanager" comes from a South American Tupi Indian word meaning "any small, brightly colored bird." The male sheds (molts) his bright-scarlet plumage in the fall, appearing more like the female during winter.

male
p. 267

female

Baltimore Oriole

Icterus galbula

SUMMER

Size: 7–8" (18–20 cm)

Female: Pale yellow with orange tones and gray-brown wings with white wing bars. Gray bill. Dark eyes.

Male: flaming orange with a black head and back, white-and-orange wing bars, an orange-and-black tail, a gray bill and dark eyes

Juvenile: same as female

Nest: pendulous; female builds; 1 brood per year

Eggs: 4–5; bluish with brown markings

Incubation: 12–14 days; female incubates

Fledging: 12–14 days; female and male feed the young

Migration: complete, to Mexico, Central America and South America

Food: insects, fruit, nectar; comes to nectar, orange-half and grape-jelly feeders

Compare: The female Orchard Oriole (p. 309) has a dull-yellow belly. Look for the gray-brown wings to identify the female Baltimore Oriole.

Stan's Notes: A fantastic songster, often heard before seen. Easily attracted to bird feeders that offer sugar water (nectar), orange halves or grape jelly. Parents bring young to feeders. Sits at the top of trees, feeding on caterpillars. Female builds a sock-like nest at the outermost branches of tall trees. Prefers parks, yards and forests and often returns to the same area year after year. Seen during migration and summer. Some of the last birds to arrive in spring (May) and some of the first to leave in the fall (September). Young males turn orange-and-black at 1½ years of age.

male
p. 269

female

first-year
male

Orchard Oriole
Icterus spurius

SUMMER MIGRATION

Size: 7–8" (18–20 cm)

Female: Olive green with a dull-yellow belly. Gray wings with 2 indistinct white wing bars. Long, thin bill with a gray mark on the lower bill.

Male: dark orange with black head, throat, upper back, wings and tail; 1 white wing bar

Juvenile: Same as female. First-year male looks like the female, with a black bib.

Nest: pendulous; female builds; 1 brood per year

Eggs: 3–5; pale blue to white, brown markings

Incubation: 11–12 days; female and male incubate

Fledging: 11–14 days; female and male feed the young

Migration: complete, to Mexico, Central America and northern South America

Food: insects, fruit, nectar; comes to nectar, orange-half and grape-jelly feeders

Compare: The female Baltimore Oriole (p. 307) has orange tones and more-distinct wing bars. The female Scarlet Tanager (p. 305) has a larger bill.

Stan's Notes: Named "Orchard" for its preference for orchards. Also likes open woods. Eats insects until wild fruit starts to ripen. Often nests alone; sometimes nests in small colonies. Parents bring their young to bird feeding stations after they fledge. Many people don't see these birds at feeders much during the summer and think they have left, but the birds are still there, hunting for insects to feed to their young. Some of the first birds to migrate at the end of summer. Often migrates in flocks with Baltimore Orioles.

male

female

juvenile

Evening Grosbeak
Coccothraustes vespertinus

WINTER

Size:	8" (20 cm)
Male:	Striking bird with bright-yellow eyebrows, rump and belly. Black-and-white wings and tail. Dark, dirty-yellow head and large, thick ivory to greenish bill.
Female:	similar to male, with softer colors and a gray head and throat
Juvenile:	similar to female, with a brown bill
Nest:	cup; female builds; 1 brood per year
Eggs:	3–4; blue with brown markings
Incubation:	12–14 days; female incubates
Fledging:	13–14 days; female and male feed the young
Migration:	irruptive; moves around in winter to find food
Food:	seeds, insects, fruit; comes to seed feeders
Compare:	The American Goldfinch (p. 293) is closely related, but it is much smaller. Look for the yellow eyebrows and thick bill to identify the Evening Grosbeak.

Stan's Notes: One of the largest finches. Characteristic finch-like undulating flight. Uses its unusually large bill to crack seeds, its main food source. Often seen on gravel roads eating gravel, which provides minerals, salt and grit to grind the seeds it eats. Sheds the outer layer of its bill during spring, exposing a blue-green bill. Moves in flocks in winter, searching for food, often visiting feeders. More numerous in some years than others. Sometimes it is totally absent. Was once a common feeder bird. Population is estimated to have declined more than 80 percent over the past 50 years.

Western
Meadowlark

Eastern Meadowlark
Sturnella magna

YEAR-ROUND
SUMMER

Size: 9" (23 cm)

Male: Robin-shaped bird with a short tail, yellow chest and belly, brown back and V-shaped black necklace. White outer tail feathers, best seen when flying away.

Female: same as male

Juvenile: same as adults

Nest: cup on the ground in dense cover; female builds; 2 broods per year

Eggs: 3–5; white with brown markings

Incubation: 13–15 days; female incubates

Fledging: 11–12 days; female and male feed the young

Migration: non-migrator to partial in Ohio, Mexico and Central America

Food: insects, seeds

Compare: The Horned Lark (p. 131) is smaller and lacks the yellow chest and belly. Look for a V-shaped black marking on the chest to help identify the Eastern Meadowlark.

Stan's Notes: A songbird of open grassy country, singing when perched and in flight. Given the name "Meadowlark" because it's a bird of meadows and sings like the larks of Europe. Best known for its wonderful, clear, flute-like whistling song. Often seen perching on fence posts but will quickly dive into tall grass when approached. Sometimes domes its nest with dried grass. Not in the lark family. A member of the blackbird family, related to grackles and orioles. Western Meadowlark (inset) is very similar but sings a different song. The map reflects the combined range of both species.

BIRDING ON THE INTERNET

Birding online is a great way to discover additional information and learn more about birds. These websites will assist you in your pursuit of birds. Web addresses sometimes change a bit, so if one no longer works, just enter the name of the group into a search engine to track down the new address.

Site	Address
Author Stan Tekiela's homepage	naturesmart.com
American Birding Association	aba.org
Audubon's Guide to Birding in Ohio	audubon.org/news/birding-ohio
The Cornell Lab of Ornithology	birds.cornell.edu
eBird's Guide to Birding in Ohio	birding-in-ohio.com
Glen Helen Raptor Center	glenhelen.org/raptor-center
Medina Raptor Center	medinaraptorcenter.org
Ohio Ornithological Society	ohiobirds.org

CHECKLIST/INDEX BY SPECIES

Use the boxes to check the birds you've seen.

OBSERVATION NOTES

OBSERVATION NOTES

OBSERVATION NOTES

The Story of AdventureKEEN

We are an independent nature and outdoor activity publisher. Our founding dates back more than 40 years, guided then and now by our love of being in the woods and on the water, by our passion for reading and books, and by the sense of wonder and discovery made possible by spending time recreating outdoors in beautiful places.

It is our mission to share that wonder and fun with our readers, especially with those who haven't yet experienced all the physical and mental health benefits that nature and outdoor activity can bring.

#bewellbeoutdoors

MORE FOR THE MIDWEST BY STAN TEKIELA

Identification Guides

Birds of Prey of the Midwest
Field Guide

Trees of Ohio Field Guide

Wildflowers of Ohio
Field Guide

Adventure Quick Guides

Birds of the Midwest

Birds of Prey of the Midwest

Water Birds of the Midwest

Wildflowers of the Midwest

Children's Books

C Is for Cardinal

Can You Count the Critters?

Critter Litter

The Kids' Guide to Birds
of Ohio

Children's Books: Adventure Board Book Series

Floppers & Loppers

Paws & Claws

Peepers & Peekers

Snouts & Sniffers

Children's Books: Wildlife Picture Books

Baby Bear Discovers the World

The Cutest Critter

Do Beavers Need Blankets?

Hidden Critters

Jump, Little Wood Ducks

Some Babies Are Wild

Super Animal Powers

What Eats That?

Whose Baby Butt?

Whose Butt?

Whose Track is That?

Wildlife Appreciation Series
Amazing Hummingbirds
Backyard Birds
Bears
Bird Migration
Cranes, Herons & Egrets
Deer, Elk & Moose
Fascinating Loons
Intriguing Owls
Lives of Wolves, Coyotes
   and Foxes
Wild Birds

Nature Appreciation Series
Bird Nests
Feathers
Wildflowers

Backyard Bird Feeding Guides
Bluebirds
Cardinals
Finches
Hummingbirds
Orioles
Woodpeckers

Our Love of Wildlife Series
Our Love of Hummingbirds
Our Love of Loons
Our Love of Owls

Audio CDs
Bird Songs of the Northwoods
Fascinating Loons: Alluring
   Sounds of the Common Loon

MORE FOR THE MIDWEST BY STAN TEKIELA

Nature Books
Bird Trivia
Start Mushrooming
A Year in Nature with Stan Tekiela

Notecards
Birds of the Heartland Notecards
Birds of the Northwoods
Notecards

Nature's Wild Cards
Birds of the Midwest
Playing Cards
Mammals of the Midwest
Playing Cards
Trees of the Midwest
Playing Cards
Wildflowers of the Midwest
Playing Cards
Hummingbirds Playing Cards
Loons Playing Cards
Owls Playing Cards
Raptors Playing Cards